*if you
love me*

"Realizing that . . . the disease of addiction is more powerful than even the very strongest parent-child bond is the essence of Cavanagh's maternal 'journey,' which will offer readers facing similar struggles some useful information and, above all, the comfort of knowing that they are not alone." —*The New York Times Book Review*

"Not since David Sheff's *Beautiful Boy* has a parent so vividly shared such a story. *If You Love Me* is intense, frightening, and also heartwarming." —**Travis Lupick, journalist and author of** ***Fighting for Space***

"Maureen Cavanagh understands, at the deepest level, the terror and the helplessness that families feel as they watch their child spiral into the void. The story that she shares in *If You Love Me* is the story of thousands, and it is told with honesty, compassion, and fierce hope. Maureen's commitment to overcoming stigma and isolation in this book will help families for years to come." —**Ruth A. Potee, MD, addictionologist**

"A frank and vivid portrayal of a mother's journey through the potentially grave and enduring unpredictability of a loved one's opioid addiction. An invaluable resource for suffering families as well as for those wishing to understand the phenomenology of the disease of addiction and, indeed, the hope of recovery and new beginnings." —**John F. Kelly, PhD, ABPP; Elizabeth R. Spallin Associate Professor of Psychiatry, Harvard Medical School; director, Recovery Research Institute, Massachusetts General Hospital**

"An emotionally fraught tale of a mother's love and her actions to save her daughter from opioid addiction." —*Kirkus Reviews*

"Cavanagh's writing is honest and straightforward, her pace fast and tone foreboding; all this makes for a page-turner that puts readers beside her on the emotional roller coaster that dealing with a loved one's substance abuse is." —*Booklist*

"Kindred spirits . . . will fully appreciate Cavanagh's stellar job in reassuring parents . . . offering subtle, in-story advice and rueful observations that make this book valuable for a parent, grandparent, friend, and politician. This book deserves its spot on a growing list of books on addiction. . . . If you need the comfort, you may want to reach for *If You Love Me* first." —*The Guam Daily Post*

if you love me

A Mother's Journey Through Her Daughter's Addiction and Recovery

Maureen Cavanagh

A Holt Paperback
Henry Holt and Company
New York

Holt Paperbacks
Henry Holt and Company
Publishers since 1866
120 Broadway
New York, New York 10271
www.henryholt.com

A Holt Paperback® and 🐸® are registered trademarks of
Macmillan Publishing Group, LLC.

The Library of Congress has cataloged the hardcover edition as follows:

Names: Cavanagh, Maureen, author.
Title: If you love me : a mother's journey through her daughter's opioid addiction / by
    Maureen Cavanagh.
Description: First edition. | New York : Henry Holt and Company, 2018.
Identifiers: LCCN 2017059765 | ISBN 9781250297341 (hardcover)
Subjects: LCSH: Cavanagh, Maureen. | Opioid abuse. | Parents of drug addicts—
    Biography. | Women drug addicts—Family relationships—Biography. | Daughters—
    Drug use. | Mothers and daughters.
Classification: LCC RC568.O45 C38 2018 | DDC 362.29092 [B]—dc23
LC record available at https://lccn.loc.gov/2017059765

ISBN 978-125-02-3454-4 (trade paperback)

Our books may be purchased in bulk for promotional, educational, or
business use. Please contact your local bookseller or the Macmillan
Corporate and Premium Sales Department at (800) 221-7945,
extension 5442, or by e-mail at MacmillanSpecialMarkets@macmillan.com.

Originally published in hardcover in 2018 by Henry Holt and Company

First Holt Paperbacks Edition 2020

Designed by Susan Walsh

This book is lovingly dedicated to Mariah Lotti and Brian Murphy, all of those who have been lost to substance use disorder, and the families and loved ones they've left behind.

May we all carry on boldly in your names.

I pray this book opens the doors of understanding and connects those lost and alone, as I tell this story in honor of each person who fights this disease, especially my Ladybug, Katie Harvey, and all of the others who have become like extended family to me.

Stay strong and know you are loved!

Contents

prologue | Winter 2017

I'm not sure how I get into the car, but I know I'm on my way to kill Bob.

I don't want to take my eyes off the road because I'm feeling unsteady and it's important I get there. I don't want to miss him. A few minutes can make all the difference. I can see in my mind's eye the bat cracking across his skull. I won't stop there. I will beat him, a man twice my size, in front of whoever is there, despite his cries for mercy, over and over, until he stops moving, stops crying out, stops destroying my beautiful Katie. I won't quit until he isn't breathing. Then I will spit on him—something I've never even considered doing to anyone in my fifty-four years of life. I will do all this and I will never have a moment's guilt over it.

I reach over and touch the top of the bat. This is long overdue.

The calm exterior that the world sees is about to shatter. This last chain of events has broken something. I know what I need to do. I can't remember the last time, during this horror show of the past two years, when I was so clear about anything. So many unanswered questions, so many late-night pleas to God, so many theories about what I did wrong—it's a relief to finally have an answer, even this one.

I feel as if the bat is also begging to kill Bob. It is my son Liam's bat. The "Golden Child," his brother and sisters call him half-jokingly.

I am lost in thought, the last of the day's sun slowly fading into dusk, and stop abruptly at a crosswalk, my arm accidentally hitting the car horn. It startles me as well as a woman crossing the street. She glares at me. Relax, lady. *I notice that her coat is buttoned incorrectly, so that her entire front is askew, with the right side of the garment riding high above the left. She's limping to the same side. I think Picasso put her together. I mouth the words "I'm sorry." She quickens her step, pulling something out of her purse. She doesn't understand what I'm saying, so I roll down the window. "I'm sorry," I say. She begins to scream, "I'm writing your license plate down, I'm going to the police, I'm going to the POLICE!"*

Is everyone walking around just about to snap? I wonder if most people are just holding themselves together by a thread. I'm grateful for being so calm. The thought that often strikes me nowadays is how little we know about what goes on in the lives of others. The face we show to the world is rarely the one we wear in private.

It's been so very long since I felt anything other than heartbroken that I'm pretty convinced it's never been any other way. I look down at my body, twenty pounds heavier. The doctor had warned me about that, two years ago, when I started to take a daily 50 milligrams of Zoloft for the paralyzing anxiety that looked a lot like sadness, but somehow the weight still snuck up on me. It's not the small pill causing the gains, I know that. It's my secret relationship with Ben and Jerry. Nothing other than Peanut Butter Cup will do, and I've hunted through store after store until I find it. Then I go home, climb into bed, watch a sitcom with a laugh track, and comfort myself with on-demand mindlessness and empty calories.

It could be worse, I tell myself. I know this is true because I've seen much, much worse. I've seen so much pain in the last few years. I hadn't known just how much pain the world could contain. It crushes me sometimes, not just my own but the pain of so many others also trying to hang on to whatever shred of their loved ones they can.

I don't know how I got here. There is never a day that goes by that this does not feel very surreal.

I can't save my daughter Katie, and sometimes that feels like the only certainty in my life. I can't make her stop using drugs any more than I could keep her from leaving any of the forty treatment centers she has left or safeguard her from the double-digit number of overdoses. I've finally come to the realization that there is nothing I can say or do that will make a real difference. She is going to leave the facility she's in now. I know because she has called and told me so. I tried to talk her out of it, saying all the things I've said a thousand times before, the things that have helped a hundred people before her, but I could hear the venom in her voice. Some switch has flipped, and she is ready to run. Not the first time, but I know it could be the last. This will be one of several treatment centers where she has been doing well and suddenly she decides to leave, courtesy of a fifty-six-year-old piece of shit named Bob.

I'm drifting to one side of the road when my phone rings and snaps me back to attention. I hope for a brief second that it will be the call, the one I've dreamed about that will tell me this is all a mistake, nothing to worry about, go home and eat your ice cream. And when I realize that this isn't happening, I wonder briefly if people on the way to kill someone answer the phone. There really isn't a rule book or protocol for this, so I reach for it and study the name of the caller.

*if you
love me*

one

Winter 2015

am waiting. Snow falls. Over five feet in February, with a record-setting ninety inches between January 24 and February 15. Lucky for me that during several of those days I was happily soaking up some vitamin D with my boyfriend, Randy, in Puerto Rico. We love it down there, the sun as opposed to snow, but also the ocean, the way we can stare out at where the sky meets the sea. While I was gone, Katie and her boyfriend, Chad, had stayed at my house, since Liam's away at college, in exchange for keeping the driveway and steps shoveled.

But now it's March, and I am the one shoveling. Or trying to. I've put my layers back on. If I don't keep the driveway and stoops cleared of accumulation every few hours, it will ice over and require a pickax to get through. As it is, there's no opening the front door, and if not for the garage door that slides up on a hinge, I would've had to jump out the window and shovel my way back to the buried entrance. Time is not on my side.

I'm hoping that one of the four men who constitute my neighbors will offer some assistance, because they have two things I don't. They all have snow blowers, and they all have wives looking out the windows, warm and toasty in their houses, patiently waiting for them. I know I should go over to one of them and ask for help, but goddamn it, I shouldn't need to. What is wrong with the people in this small town northeast of Boston? Back in New York, specifically Long Island, where I grew up, this wouldn't happen. My girlfriends back home would be out here with a shovel, too, and no one would head back home until everyone was shoveled out. They can't possibly think I don't need their help?

Fuck them, I think, stepping deeper into the whiteness.

After an hour, I'm the only person out there in the dark. There is that stillness that occurs only when snow is falling. I can hear a plow scraping the road in the distance. I hold my breath each time it gets closer, knowing that eventually I'll be blocked in again and that the new barrier may be the thing that sends me screaming out into the road to throw myself under the next snowplow. Katie is snowed in by this time herself, a town away, with her boyfriend, so they can't help. With Randy buried in snow at his own house, twenty miles away, I'm it, I'm all I've got. Shoveling snow up and onto a fifteen-foot ridge at the side of the driveway. Every time I turn around, the spot I shoveled is covered again. I feel the tears freezing on my face as I rest my forehead on the handle of the shovel.

"Fuck me," I say, first quietly and then a little louder. Liam has often commented that this is what I should have written on my tombstone. It's appropriate that I am saying it now, because it'll directly precede the stroke I feel like I'm about to have.

I look up to see, in the distance, a young black man with a snow shovel. Shaking my head, I wonder if imagining diversity in this "couldn't get any whiter" town is a sign of hypothermia. He smiles, clearly having heard my outburst, and says the four most beautiful words in the English language:

"Do you need help?"

Not giving it a second thought, he starts to shovel.

I can't stop thanking him. Martin is his name. It's nothing, Martin keeps telling me. He is young, maybe twenty, and strong. He makes more progress in ten minutes than I've made in an hour. Martin lives up the street and was heading over to help a friend dig out when he saw me. Martin is not as surprised as I am that my neighbors haven't helped me.

His phone rings, and he quickly answers it with a hurried "Yeah, yeah, yeah man," and he promises to come back and finish when he's done helping his friend. He tells me to go inside and leave the shovel on the steps because mine is better than the ragged one he has been using. Realizing that being a Good Samaritan in the moment is one thing but expecting him to return is another, I watch as Martin walks down the middle of the empty street. The curtain of snow falls after him.

"Good-bye, Martin," I whisper.

The driveway is covered in white again.

I head back into the house. I don't care anymore. I am beaten by the snow, the town, and life. I officially give up, throw down my snow shovel. Well, I leave it on the porch, convinced that it's more likely to be stolen by the end of the night than used again by me. Good, I've had enough. I'm never shoveling that white shit again. They can come and wheel me out in the spring.

At age nine, in 1972, when George McGovern was running for president, I wrote him letters and passed out leaflets in hopes of helping him get elected. I wrote to the Kennedys about saving the whales. I rescued animals: turtles, cats, and geese. I nursed a cat back to health that was half-dead when I found it. As I close the door on all that snow and shrug out of my parka, I try to think back to a time when I didn't feel overwhelmed and alone. I can't. A textbook child of an alcoholic, I typically feel it necessary to worry about and take care of everyone except myself.

Most of all, I worry about Katie. I love her so much. She had a bout with anorexia and depression in her mid-teens and had been doing well—until the most recent car accident in a series of minor accidents that always seem to rattle her and derail her progress. To put it mildly, she is a terrible driver who won't wear her glasses, which only makes her more terrible. The best drive of her life must have been during her driving test. She's hit two curbs, multiple parked cars, and clipped a few on the road. We blame it on depth perception.

Last year, when she stopped her college classes because she was worried she had been drinking too much and experimenting with drugs, we quietly found an outpatient program. She had been hanging around a local kid name Gabe Wright and I thought he was the cause, so she agreed to stay away from him. Knowing he is out of the picture, I feel reassured. She's now twenty-two, supposedly an adult, and she tells me she is doing well.

I miss Katie. I miss the long walks around Marblehead we took, the bits of gossip from school and her job in the local grocery store, and just watching bad television in bed with her. Katie has been staying with her boyfriend, who goes to a local college, while she completes classes to be an aesthetician, getting rides back and forth now that her car is out of commission. I tell myself that there are reasons she is never home: school, work, and the damn New England snow. So many different stories I tell myself. Deep down, I've noticed a change I don't like. I push it out of my head. I give her another chance to prove to me that she's okay. I watch and I wait.

The sound of scraping pulls me back into the present. I wonder if the plow has finally come to deal me its death blow, so I open the door.

"Don't worry," Martin says. "Stay inside."

The wind has picked up but the snow has stopped, and he promises to have it done before I know it.

"Martin, your mother raised a good man," I call out to him. "Please knock on the door when you're done."

I go back in and make myself a cup of tea and promise myself a hot bath as soon as he is finished shoveling. Always dieting, I decide to treat myself to a spoonful of honey but, once again, can't find any spoons, not one. I think of all those socks that disappear in the wash and imagine that there is a special place in heaven for them and the spoons.

In the secret stash of emergency cash in the back of my drawer, I'm somehow down to a single twenty. Emptying the bills out of my wallet, I count all the money I have in the house. Whatever it is, I'm giving it to Martin.

The moment when Martin saved me is the last happy one I can remember before everything changed.

Everywhere across Massachusetts people are almost giddy that it hasn't snowed in several days. Snow is piled high above my head on both sides of the driveway, a narrow ravine cut in the mountainous snowbank so that I can pull the car in and out. I'm excited to be going out tonight after way too much time alone lately.

I am the sort of person who puts on earrings and a necklace on Tuesday and a month and half later, I'm wearing the same jewelry. I just don't think about it. It's not that I don't like accessories, it just never crosses my mind to change them. When I was younger, I had a friend who owned more costume jewelry than Macy's. At that point in my life, I had none.

"Put some earrings and a necklace on, for Christ's sake," she said one day. "You look like I just picked you up from prison."

Lacking a desire to look like I'd done a stint at Rikers, I tried to get hip, but I still rarely think to change anything unless I'm going somewhere special. Tonight, assuming the roads are okay, I am going somewhere special. Randy and I are going out on a real date.

On the center of my dresser for many years there has been a cloth-covered jewelry box filled with a few nice things. The box is falling apart, but I can't bear to replace it. Looking at it, I remember the Christmas shopping trip when Katie and Liam purchased it. At seven and four, they had scraped up a little bit of money from doing chores that didn't really need to be done and asked if they could go shopping alone to buy me a present. But since I was divorced with four kids in a state where I knew few people, I had no one else who could take them. So, I drove them to Target, which we fondly pronounced with a French accent, and trailed behind them, promising I wasn't looking. Katie watched carefully so that her brother didn't fall behind or break anything.

I can still see the adorable little scene as if it happened yesterday. Finally, and I do mean finally, because we circle the store approximately nine hundred times, they make it to the cash register. The woman in line behind them sees that I'm watching them and catches on, winking at me. There's a little commotion. As Liam attempts to put a packet of Reese's Peanut Butter Cups on the conveyor, panic sets across Katie's face. She doesn't have enough money. The woman behind them in line whispers something to Katie, taking two dollars out of her wallet, then extracts another single and pushes the candy toward the cashier. She turns to me and shakes her head as I try to approach with my wallet open.

Still shaking her head, she mouths the words "My pleasure."

I mouth back my thanks and slip through an empty cashier aisle so that I can catch up with the two of them, both beaming with pride. I turn and wave to the woman now paying for her own purchases and am so filled with gratitude for my life and the kindness of people I don't even know that I'm sure I'll never forget her gesture.

So, I keep the things that are important to me in this little box covered with flowers and sequins, even though it is slowly disintegrating, because I like knowing that whatever is inside the box could never be as important as the box itself.

I decide to put on my good earrings, because if I don't do it while I'm thinking about it, I won't remember later. I open my little box and look for the one really nice pair of diamond earrings I own. Semicircles just big enough but not too big and covered with little diamonds. Grown-up jewelry mixed in with dime-store things the kids have given me over the years. I pick up the top compartment and search underneath, not seeing them where they normally sit.

They're not here.

I look again in the same spot and then again. I take everything out and lay it on the dresser. It is at first a mild disbelief, something like how, when I do the dishes, I keep wondering where all my spoons have gone. My hands are starting to shake, and I feel nauseous. I notice the absence of the few other pieces of jewelry worth something. My great-grandmother's teardrop pearl necklace, which I wore when I got married. A necklace from an old boyfriend who had good taste in jewelry, that being his only redeeming quality.

A thought like a black cloud sweeps over me. Standing at my dresser, earrings, bracelets, and necklaces spread out across the wooden surface, I bow my head and pray for something awful: "Please, God, please let me have been robbed by a stranger." If I've been robbed by a stranger, then across the small bedroom in a dresser where I keep papers and bits of nothing, in the third drawer from the bottom, where no one would look unless they knew where to look, all the way in the back of that drawer, there will still be the family jewelry that I never wear. My mother's engagement ring, which I was given after she died. The rings my father took off and handed to me the night he passed away. The engagement ring my ex-husband had spent months saving for, running to the jeweler near the bar where he worked anytime he had extra money, to build up his deposit.

"Please, God, please don't let this be true," I beg as I make my way across the room.

I pause for a moment to gaze at the painting hanging over the slim white dresser, the dresser that holds the answer to my question. Hundreds of tiny yellow flowers with mountains in the background. Katie painted it in her senior year of high school. I want so badly to go back in time. Back to when I took for granted that Katie would finish college, marry her high school boyfriend, and raise a family, or some version of that story. Back to when I sat on the edge of the bed and showed her the jewelry I would eventually pass on to her.

Cautiously, I open the drawer, moving the paperwork aside. I fall to my knees, lifting the lids of boxes, and look at the emptiness over and over until my brain processes exactly what has happened.

The only valuable items left in the drawer are the things Randy has given me over the last few years. Only one person in my world would know which were which.

When I explain Katie to people, I always tell the story of her reaction to my mother's death. My mother and I were never close, to put it kindly, and her death, not long after I moved back east from

Utah, was not a surprise. Still, it was unsettling to have the person who brought me into the world gone, and I gave myself some time before I told my children. First, I told the older set, Melody, sixteen, and her brother Ryan, fourteen. They took it pretty well. I was less sure about my younger two kids. I bought a book by Maria Shriver about explaining death to children and told them Nanny had gone to heaven, not completely believing that myself. Liam, at five years old, had very little reaction to the news of her passing, but Katie, at eight, immediately gasped.

I thought she was about to burst into tears, but instead she said, "Oh no, if I'm this upset, imagine how sad you must be."

That is Katie.

Now, as I stand in front of the dresser, my thoughts go back to the long weekend in February when I'd left Katie and Chad at my house to keep the driveway clear of snow while I was away. After I'd returned, while waiting for Martin to finish shoveling me out, I had found a spoon at the bottom of the dishwasher. It was bent and burnt. I had chalked its condition up to its having been used to fix something I wasn't supposed to know had broken. As I recall all of this, a wave of sickness comes over me.

I pick up the phone and call Katie.

"Hi, Mommy," she says happily.

Even then, I realize that this is the last time I will ever hear her sound so innocent. This conversation will change everything between us. I am going to accuse her of stealing my jewelry, and it will be true, and there will be an excuse that neither one of us will like.

"My jewelry is gone, and I know that you took it."

Katie breaks down sobbing. "I'm so sorry, it was killing me. I am so sorry. I'm trying to get it back. I love you."

"Come home right now," I tell her.

I honestly can't think of anything else to say. I hang up and call her father and tell him the same thing.

It's not the missing jewelry that breaks my heart. It's knowing that her life has spiraled so far out of control that she would *need* to do this to me and to herself. I have no idea what her life has become, which means I have no idea how bad this will get. Over the next few months, I'll find other things missing as I go to use them. A spare television I had given her, her computer, silver flatware, medication, a punching bag of her brother's. The empty spaces where these things were stand as reminders of the destruction.

Katie arrives before long and sits on the couch in her too-large coat looking small, vulnerable, dirty, and sick. She was dropped off by Chad, and he waits for her, like a coward, slightly down the street.

She starts to cry and apologize, and the words float over me. She took everything the weekend I was in Puerto Rico. Two separate visits to the pawnshop. She got a couple hundred bucks for over thirty thousand dollars' worth of my lifetime of treasures and memories. I'm not even sure what to say. I'm not angry, I'm stunned. Did this happen overnight, or did I somehow not see what was in front of me?

We wait for her father, my ex-husband, Mike, as if he has the answer about what to do next. He and I have come a long way, and even with that, it's still far from an easy relationship. I dreaded making the phone call to him and am not looking forward to his reaction. We sit in silence in the house where Katie has spent much of her childhood. Purchasing this house on my own was one of the biggest accomplishments of my life. I sold everything when I left Utah, including a commercial janitorial service I'd started, initially cleaning offices at night with Liam strapped on my front in a baby carrier, then growing it to employ a dozen workers. To take advantage of a fellowship at Suffolk University, in Boston, I moved across the country, newly divorced and with four kids, to start over. I had squirreled away enough money to buy a house, without anything left over for furniture, in a beautiful town with good schools. I was going to give my children the life they deserved.

I spent the first year recovering from pouring everything I had into the down payment: our bare living room became what I called the Olympic Sock-Skating Center. Putting on our thickest socks, we'd use the gleaming hardwood floors for competitions on how far we could slide, or we'd just do laps around the tiny empty living room. A chill runs up and down my back now as we sit in the fully furnished room: how far we have come from those days only a short time ago. But I'd give it all away to have it empty again, save for my sock-skating Katie.

At this moment, sitting on the couch, she looks like a lost child waiting for her mother to collect her after going missing at Walmart. Her big brown eyes are red from crying, and her mascara has settled underneath them. Her hair is a mess. Naturally a beautiful chestnut that hangs to her midback, it's been dyed black and pulled up in a clip at the nape of her neck. Nothing about her resembles the girl who would literally have stopped traffic just a few short months ago.

When Mike arrives, he looks exactly how I must look to him: completely and utterly crushed. The news has aged Mike twenty years. He sits down in the living room and holds his head in his hands. I'm afraid that when he lifts his face, he will be crying. Though he is normally strong and forceful, there is a little boy inside that tough exterior of the man.

Katie tells us a story about how her boyfriend is trying to get the jewelry back. She can't stop relating every detail. The pawnshop, the Craigslist ads, meeting people so that they can hand over what was mine in exchange for drugs and small amounts of cash. She starts repeating herself. She is high. I don't know how I hadn't noticed it before, but it is glaringly obvious now.

We demand to see her arms. And this I am not expecting; if I had known, I wouldn't have demanded.

Track marks, unmistakable, crisscross her flesh. My sweet girl who would lay her arm across my lap and plead, "Tickle me," is marked with the telltale signs of heroin use. I feel all the air rush out of my lungs, and in its absence, the truth hits me again like a sledgehammer.

Why did I have to see this, so undeniable, to finally understand what had been going on? The changes I could have noticed but didn't: her sweet personality shifting from loving to moody. Just a teenager, I said. Friends that changed, the new people she hung out with, her hair, which she had dyed, pulled back, and stopped combing. Certainly just a phase. Plastic caps in the laundry that I thought were caps from electrical work. Lighters lying around that were said to belong to "friends," even though no one smoked. Sleeping all day and staying out too late. I attributed it all to school, depression, anything. How could I be so blind? Although it's taken years, it's only now, in a moment, that the fog lifts and I recognize what is in front of me.

Her father wants to know who dragged her into this. The shock is fading, and he is angry. Angry works for him. Mike is a corrections officer in the state prison system. You would never know that this big guy with a shaved head, tattoos, and an angry expression permanently fixed on his face is the same sweet man who paid off my engagement ring each week for months.

"Was it Gabe?" he asks.

Katie's older brother, Ryan, had warned us about Gabe Wright when she first started hanging out with him. Ryan is very protective of his little sister, and he'd heard that Gabe Wright was into drugs.

"Was it Chad?" I ask.

I never liked him; he was sloppy and lazy, without the decent manners to say hello or good-bye when in my house.

"Is he doing this, too?"

"Yes."

I look out the window and see that Chad has left. There is an overwhelming desire to blame someone, something, anything—anyone other than her. How will I fix this if it's her that is the problem?

Our sweet little blond-haired toddler had stood in the window every night waiting for her daddy to come home, giving new words to the theme music of *Jeopardy!*—"Daddy, Daddy, I love you"—while she waited patiently for him to pull into the driveway.

As a three-year-old, she'd followed all the neighborhood kids on our street while they rollerbladed, swinging her arms and frolicking in her sneakers that lit up, looking like the happiest of the bunch, never realizing it was necessary to have wheels on her feet.

My nine-year-old, dangerously close to puberty but still a little girl, had performed in the church choir after practicing long and hard to sing her Sunday morning solo, "Morning Has Broken," from the balcony. Her sweet voice filled the church while I told everyone around me and several pews over that she was my daughter, my eyes brimming over with tears. My heart swelled with love and pride.

My teenager, when she was still young enough to make time to walk with her mom through our historic town, past century-old homes and mansions on the water, had loved playing Which House Do You Want to Live In?

My high school graduate, walking across the stage to get her diploma, had surprised everyone by winning a scholarship and making the honor roll, although she'd struggled with a learning disability that had forced her to work twice as hard as everyone else.

My Ladybug.

I wonder if she is still in there, that girl. She must be. I must find her, uncover her, release her. I can't reconcile my daughter with the person nodding off in front of me. The magnitude of the situation hits me again and again.

She puts her coat back on, asking for her phone, which I had taken earlier.

"You're not going anywhere, Katie. You're going to treatment."

"Oh yeah? Where?" she spits out, aware that I have no idea.

"I don't know. You know people who use drugs. You must know someone who has gone to treatment. Where did they go?"

The irony of this is not lost on anyone.

I look at Mike. He has no idea what to do with her, either.

"I have a friend who went to Florida, and he's doing well now. You know, the kid who hit the tree and flipped his car last year," she explains matter-of-factly.

"Patrick Ryan? Dear God, he does heroin? Oh, my God. What's the name of the place?"

She tells us and immediately follows that by adding that she can't leave Chad.

She nods off again, sleeping, sitting straight up, head hanging to one side.

"What the hell are we going to do?" I ask Mike, fully aware that he doesn't have a clue.

"I say we just call the fucking cops on the two of them. Report them for stealing your jewelry. And let the police cart them off to jail."

"Well, that would be a felony. You're thinking a couple of years in Framingham might be good for her?" I try desperately to hold my tongue and not have another of the million fights every divorced couple has that remind them why they are no longer married.

"I don't know. No, of course not. I don't know what to do. Google something—there must be information online. Isn't there someone we can ask for help?"

"Can we just call the police and ask what to do? You're a corrections officer—don't you know?"

Mike explains the little he can remember about a legal way to get her into treatment even if she doesn't want to go. "I don't really know exactly how to do it," he says, "but I know we need to go to court and that it doesn't happen immediately. If we hold her here against her will, that's kidnapping, and if we report the theft, she will go to jail, so the only thing left is threatening her with getting arrested so that she will go somewhat willingly."

"What happens if she won't go?"

There's no good answer to that question. She can do what she wants. At twenty-two, she's an adult. Before I can start looking at our in-network providers, Katie picks up the conversation exactly where we left off, bolt upright. I explain to her that if she moves a muscle off the couch, I'll call the police and report the theft.

"I don't care what happens to me. You can't make me go anywhere."

In my calmest voice possible, I explain that unless she wants both herself and Chad to be arrested, she will go to a treatment center. I remind her how well Chad would do in jail, and her father chimes in to add that he will personally see to it that Chad will never forget the experience. She begins to cry.

I comfort myself with the knowledge that as bad as this is, at least no one knows. My neighbors can continue to plow their own snowflakes, never needing to look over the fence, never knowing what is going on next door—here, now. Katie can recover from this, and we will look back on it as a bad patch in an otherwise good life. She has the support and love of her family, and we are coming together around her. We will stick by her. Mike and I can still fix this. I have no idea how, but as long as no one knows, we can get past this.

We dig in, argue, and by the end of the day, we have her scheduled for detox followed by a twenty-eight-day treatment program, both located in Massachusetts. Katie sits on the couch waiting to go, nodding off again. The horrible thing is that I've seen her nod off like this many times over the past few months, and I've repeatedly told her to stop hanging out so late with her friends or to eat better, because no one else her age is that tired all the time.

When Mike takes her to the detox facility later that evening, I try desperately not to look at the dresser and the sweet little jewelry box, but they haunt me. I tell no one because no one needs to know. They won't understand. Plus, we will fix it anyhow, so why ruin her reputation? I just have to keep her away from the people she's been hanging around. That boyfriend and Gabe Wright. None of this would have happened if not for them.

How did I not see this? What do I do now? I relive every time over the last few years when something happened that could have been a chance to intervene before it got to this point. I torture myself with all the things I could have done and the signs I should have detected.

I lie alone in bed that night, sleepless and scared. I have now read enough on the Internet that I understand that we may have a fight ahead of us, but I also know my daughter. She, too, is a fighter. I think of Martin and the snow, and how things turned around when I least expected them to. I hope that I have some leftover luck still to claim.

I fall asleep believing that Katie is different. She can be the one who conquers this quickly. I will help her.

We've got this.

two | Spring

Saucer magnolias are bursting into vibrant pink blossoms along Commonwealth Avenue, and the smell of lilacs fills my own backyard. Azaleas and rhododendrons come back to life in the tidy yards all over the North Shore of Massachusetts. Children restlessly wait for summer oblivion. Parents make vacation plans. Mothers push their babies in carriages after the long, snowy winter. Windows are opened, cross-breezes blowing back cotton curtains. And garage sales—that final phase of spring cleaning. The cheers of a Little League game go up in the distance. Lawn mowers buzz. Everywhere life is in renewal and rebirth, and my daughter Katie is missing.

For the first time in her life, I have no idea where she is. At all. She finished detox and reluctantly completed a twenty-eight-day program in Massachusetts, but she ran from a beautiful sober living facility in Portland, Maine, that I'd hoped would offer her a fresh start—where I'd brought two hundred dollars' worth of her favorite things to eat, somehow thinking that if she had enough raspberries she would stay put—and now every night I lie awake in a cold sweat, imagining people hurting her. Torturing her in a never-ending variety of ways and dumping her body in ravines, off the highway, in dumpsters. I picture her overdosing in a gas station bathroom, left blue until some overly caffeinated traveler finds her.

I become a detective. The owner of the beautiful facility, an expert on escapes, got the license plate number of the car she left in. It is not much, but it is something. Luckily, it is something I can work with. Using a perk of one of my most recent employment incarnations—selling insurance products to motorcycle dealers—I call up a friend, who runs the license plate. It doesn't take long to track down Steven, who, when confronted with my knowledge of him, says he took Katie someplace in Quincy.

I have an address now. Not a name or an apartment number, but I am getting closer. Or, I should say, "we are." My ex-husband is a detective, too, and we're standing outside Chad's last known residence when the door swings open.

"Who the fuck are you?" Mike shouts.

Mike and I met at the Queens restaurant where we both worked, he as a bartender and me as a waitress. It took months and the strong encouragement of a coworker, but he finally asked me out. He had left Dublin for the United States only a few years before, and he wore the telltale "I'm Irish and new here" white socks with dress pants when we first started dating. He'd later tell people that he was so shy that when he came to my house, he'd knock on the door with a sponge. I still have no idea what that means, but it was adorable then, and it still is. He immigrated via the back door from Ireland, overstaying a vacation by a couple of years, along with many others in the mid-eighties, drawn by the strong economy and the multitude of off-the-books jobs paying three and four times what anyone could earn in

Ireland, if they could even find a job. The bars and restaurants in Forest Hills were full of the Irish, both the workers and the drinkers, and he couldn't go anywhere without running into someone he knew from either the bar where he worked or back home or both.

Mike is an imposing figure. He used to have a quick temper I wasn't fond of, and when he drank he did so to excess. It was not a good combination. But among the close-knit group of people working the Irish bars, Mike was known as the guy you could count on if you were in trouble.

I had grown up surrounded by drugs, alcohol, and mental health issues. I was the only person I knew who had a grandmother who attended a methadone clinic after becoming addicted to painkillers. The police were at my house on a regular basis, taking one parent or the other away after yet another drunken fight. My parents lost custody of me at sixteen, and I spent time living in a group home until my mother left yet again and I was able to go back home for a short while, finishing school a year early, after the eleventh grade.

There was no way I was going to get seriously involved with anyone with a drinking problem.

I told Mike that while I cared very much for him, I couldn't be with an alcoholic. He started going to therapy and AA meetings, and he never drank again. I was amazed and overjoyed, and this confirmed for me what I had always believed: if my parents had loved me, they would have stopped.

I thought he was old-fashioned and sweet, more like someone who'd fallen out of another era. He wanted a home and a family, and it wasn't long before I found myself wanting them, too. Several years later, when he was sworn in as an American citizen, only months after Katie was born, we were well on our way.

Fast-forward twenty-two years: no longer young and no longer married, and we're standing on the porch of a house where Chad may or may not live.

"Who the fuck are you?" Mike shouts at the college roommate who has just woken up at three in the afternoon. The guy stands in the doorway wearing Salem State sweatpants and a white T-shirt that looks like it hasn't seen the inside of a washing machine since freshman year. He dumbly glances around to be sure he is, in fact, standing in his own apartment.

I suspect we have an accounting major who has most of his altercations on Xbox, not in the street, because he looks like he may wet himself. He pushes his glasses up on his nose nervously as he leans back and peers at me and then Mike and squeaks out a name I can't hear.

"Where's that piece of shit Chad? Tell me where they are or I'll wring your skinny neck."

"Michael, relax," I plead.

Behind that tough guy exterior is a heartbroken father who I worry is overdue for a heart attack or beating the crap out of someone. I'm not sure which will come first. I can tell this is not going to end well for Mervin, or Myron, or whoever he just said he was.

Mervin gathers all his courage to step away from Mike, who's now only inches from his face, and points at the empty room to the left of the entrance. There is a metal folding chair in the center of the room and trash in the corner. An ashtray sits on the chair. Aside from that, it is empty.

"He's not here. I swear. I haven't seen him in over a week. They moved everything out while I was in class."

Dead end. When I can't find Katie in person, I seek her out online. I have become dependent upon my phone—on checking it. I used to use Facebook to stay in touch with high school friends, but now it becomes my only means of communication with Katie.

"Please at least let me know you're alive," I message her.

"I'm fine Mom," she replies.

Really? I want to say. *You really must be on drugs if you think I believe that.* I remind myself that this is, in fact, true. I hold it in and take a deep breath.

Work has become an afterthought. The insurance business I built is suffering. Before this nightmare fully began, when Katie was still struggling with an eating disorder and I believed we were getting that under control, I'd left my job as a special education teacher to start an insurance business and a nonprofit. It wasn't the first time I decided to change careers. I'd booked bands into CBGB in New York in the 1980s, run a nonprofit that brought children from Northern Ireland to the States for six weeks in the summer, and later owned a commercial janitorial service, along with moving through a variety of other completely divergent jobs. I am known to be audacious or without enough sense to be afraid of starting over—depends on who you are asking. No one was surprised by my change of jobs again, although some people did question my sanity. I incorporated the business and the nonprofit, Magnolia New Beginnings, at the same time, with the hope of helping people who needed a fresh start and giving myself one in the bargain. The mission was a little vague at first, but I was sure it would evolve.

Only now there just isn't enough time to both work and worry about Katie. I forget to pay bills, send in claims, respond to texts. On a good day, when I hear from Katie, I try to get as much done as possible. On the bad days, when there is only silence, I can't hold a thought together long enough to finish a sentence. I am constantly looking at Messenger because it shows the last time she was online, and I can console myself with the fact that she was indeed alive two hours ago, forty-two minutes ago, right now. I live with the phone in my hand. I sleep with it next to my head. I take it into the shower with me, keeping it high up. I feel everything I've worked for slipping through my fingers, but I have no idea what to do differently.

I beg her to let me help her. I don't get angry. I know that each time I speak to her, each message I send could be the last. I'm too heartbroken to be angry anyhow. I live on pins and needles. My relationships are taking a beating. My other children are left behind. I find it impossible to concentrate. I'm drowning, and each time I come up for air, I get hit with another wave. There is such a temptation to let go and go under, but I won't let myself, for fear of what will happen to Katie.

I never forget what's happening. I am reminded of it constantly. Driving out of Marblehead, I see a young woman jogging along the causeway toward the beach who looks just like Katie. My heart leaps in my chest. I cruise past the grocery store where she worked for four years and recall the many times she left, coffee in hand, in her blue supermarket jacket with her name in script on the pocket, always running five minutes late, never forgetting to tell me she loved me. My problems follow me as I drive past the statue of Nathaniel Hawthorne near the Salem Common, where Katie, Liam, and I used to do an annual cancer walk together. Now Katie is everywhere and nowhere.

I try to push away that gnawing feeling of doom I carry around with me to enjoy a few days free of worry with Randy on Cape Cod for Memorial Day weekend. It isn't going well. I haven't heard from Katie in days, and I'm never able to concentrate. A quick stop for groceries, and as we make our way through the aisles I am lost in thought; all the what-ifs keep playing themselves out in my head. It is like some-one following me while steadily pounding a drum—*what if she's dead, what if she needs you, what if you can help, what if she's being hurt*—without missing a beat.

Midway through the shopping trip, in the produce department, my phone rings, and I nearly jump out of my skin. My thoughts collide. It's the mother of a friend of Liam's. *Dear God, she never calls me. He must be dead. I shouldn't be so far away. Maybe it's Katie. She's dead. It will take me hours to get home. How will I tell Liam?*

The phone rings for the second time and I sprint toward the front door, not really knowing why or what I'm running toward or away from, answering, "Is everything okay?"

"Hi, Maureen, this is Mary, how are you?"

"Good, good. Is everything okay?"

"Yes, fine," she responds, clearly sensing that she has set off a time bomb. "I was just calling to see if you and Randy had plans for the weekend."

I burst into tears outside the Stop & Shop, still holding an overly ripe avocado that I have created an impression of my hand in.

Fortunately, Mary is one of the few people who know our situation. Liam has confided in her on one of the many days and nights he has spent at her house. It feels a little uncomfortable knowing she knows, but I'm glad my son has had someone other than me to talk about his sister with. Mary is kind and understanding and she loves him. Just as importantly, I'm sure she won't tell anyone. I can't risk people finding out. If this passes quickly for Katie, it will just be a rough patch; if word gets out in this small town, I worry it will follow Katie forever.

I calm down and briefly tell Mary where we are spending the weekend and why I'm acting like a lunatic, then head back into the store, avocado in hand, to try to explain why my eyes are red and why I've left Randy holding a bag of lettuce.

He's in the checkout line, clearly annoyed or maybe just tired of this, as I am.

"It was just Mary," I relate.

There really isn't anything else to say. I get it. I really do. I am doing my very best to carry on, but it's like swimming with a hundred pounds of bricks strapped to my back.

He knows that this will continue throughout the weekend, that I'll be on edge. No matter how hard I try, I'll watch my phone for a Facebook message. We pull into the parking lot of the condo complex in Brewster, a small, lovely town full of summer homes, ponds, and easy access to Pleasant Bay. He gets out of the car and grabs the groceries. Trying to be helpful, I say I'll put them away and Randy walks up the stairs to the bedroom. This is not a good sign. It's the harbinger of a very long, icy weekend unless I can snap out of how I'm feeling and he can shake off his mood.

I get the bags unpacked and sit in a chair that looks out on a small yard. I try to relax, fiddling with my new earrings, the pair Randy bought me after Katie stole my favorite ones. Within days he had purchased diamond semicircle hoops; he gave them to me over dinner one night. "This is the beginning of replacing everything you lost," he told me. I'd never be able to replace the sentimental value of the jewelry, but the gesture broke my heart and healed it at the same time.

There is a birdbath that needs to be filled. From my oversized white chair, I watch the birds and note any new ones in our *Birds of Massachusetts* book. The damn squirrel has eaten all of the birdseed again. Outside, next to the wicker loveseat, is the submachine gun–style water pistol that I shoot the squirrels with to no avail, while they relentlessly swing from the bottom of the feeder, trying to shake lose the seeds. I relate to them.

I take a deep breath and try to relax. I wonder briefly, knowing the answer before I ask the question, if I should go upstairs and try to repair the day. *Leave him alone for a while,* my wise inner self answers. I wonder how much more of this he can take. I've seen marriages disintegrate over this kind of thing, and I think how easy it would be for him to walk away, yet he stays. He cares for Katie. They had begun to get into a routine of running 5Ks together. My heart would be so full as I watched two people I loved so much coming across the finish line. Now I worry that this will never happen again.

Instinctively, I pick up my phone. Opening Facebook, I see there are no messages, which could be either good or bad. I look at Katie's Facebook page and notice that there are no new posts. Back to Messenger, where I note that she has not been online since yesterday: decidedly not good.

As I'm scrolling through my email, a subject line from the Marblehead Patch catches my eye. My first and immediate response is how sad. How very sad. I wonder who it could be.

I read on. According to the *Salem News*, the e-mail says,

Twenty-three-year-old Kaitlin Harvey was arrested last Wednesday after she negotiated a half-hour of sexual activity with an undercover detective.

Police found an ad Harvey posted for sexual services on the website Backpage under the heading for "escort services."

The name sounds familiar, but I can't place it. I look back at the headline: "Marblehead Honor Student Arrested for Prostitution."

I read it again. And again. I stop breathing and run up the stairs two steps at a time. I revert back to my eight-year-old self and stutter, pushing the phone at Randy. "Oh, my God," I begin to repeat. I have no other words.

The sun shines through the skylight onto the bed. A breeze causes the blinds to flutter. I try to breathe and hear myself repeating "Oh my God" over and over. Why is there no air in the room when I can clearly see it flowing in? I am still trying to figure out a way that this isn't true, that it isn't her. I can't wrap my head around it all. My daughter Katie.

I'm sure the reporter is some summer intern from an overpriced college with visions of journalistic grandeur, but if she had one ounce of sense or integrity she would know there's a larger story here and what she has done may very well have ruined a young woman's life. Sex is salacious, but sex for money to buy heroin is dirty. Of course drugs are behind this. This idiot doesn't mention that. In a town this small, there is no doubt that word is already spreading like wildfire. I have seen it before, like a game of Telephone. How could the editors print this shit? This small local newspaper is acting like the *National Enquirer*. The unfairness of exposing Katie like this makes me sick. It's disgusting. I look at the name of the person who wrote the article so that I can direct my anger at someone.

The article states that Katie had posted her own bail, so I sit on the edge of the bed with my head between my knees and call her, fully expecting to get her voice mail. To my surprise, she answers. She does not even sound bad.

"I know you were arrested," I say flatly, sucking in any emotion and moving to the window. Everything is normal outside. How can that be? The squirrel swings from the bottom of the bird feeder.

"Please tell me you are willing to go back to treatment?"

Sobbing, she apologizes but doesn't agree to come home, divulge her whereabouts, or go back to treatment.

"Does Chad know about this?" I ask. "Damnit, answer me."

Her silence confirms that not only does he know but he is benefitting from her exploiting herself. That is how they are both paying for their drug use.

I need to tell my other children before they read the story in the paper or someone shares the news with them. I start with Liam, the closest to Katie and the only one still living in Marblehead. He is working in Salem, the next town over, at a restaurant popular with tourists and locals alike, saving his summer wages for his college expenses. The arrest was also in the Salem paper, and once he goes in tonight, he will be surrounded with people who have read the article.

He is stoic. I tell him I'll come home and he assures me that he is fine. He's scheduled to work a double, and he has no intention of calling in sick.

I'm worried. This is the sister he idolized. Three years apart in age, they were always inseparable. He'd crawl out of his crib, wearing his favorite pajamas with a Batman cape, and sneak into bed with her, no matter how hard I tried to keep him in his own room. She'd wake with the cape tangled around her face but would never get angry or annoyed; she acted like it was all a gift. Her baby brother could do no wrong. She saved him once in the middle of the night when he choked on a penny he had taken to bed with him. She'd adored him since the moment he was born, and the sentiment was reciprocated.

Liam has taken all his frustrations over her absence this year out in the gym, sometimes going twice a day. He's a gentle kid but at nineteen has become a muscular man who, though he wouldn't hurt a fly, appears like he could punch an angry hornets' nest. I'm worried how he will react if someone says anything to him about his sister.

I move on to my older children to let them know what has happened. They are upset, concerned, and, I sense, embarrassed. They, too, will need to deal with local friends and gossip, but they take this far more personally than their younger brother did. Later I'll ask Liam if anyone said anything to him about Katie, knowing how boys that age and people in general can be.

"They better fucking not. She's my sister," he says. He is crushed, but he sticks by her.

Days later, in an act of bravery that astounds me to this day, Katie writes to the *Marblehead Reporter* about the article about her, and the editors post her statement online:

> I'm really embarrassed over the article written about me. I'm really sorry to all my friends and family I've hurt through this nasty heroin addiction, and I hope one day I officially beat it. Thank you guys for your support.
>
> Maybe if people read that they will understand the pain addicts go thru on a daily basis. . . . I would just like people to know addicts are good people who believe they need to do bad things because they don't deserve any better.

That last sentence hurts me every time I read it because it's so resigned and weary you know she means it completely. Several people post comments under the article. They are disgusted that the newspaper has reported the story in this way. People write encouraging comments and prayers for Katie, and this kindness fuels my desire to speak up. To speak out like Katie.

But I am surrounded by silence. I hear next to nothing. One person, Mary, Liam's friend's mother, reaches out to me and to Liam. One person. She is kind, as I knew she would be, and concerned about the effect on Liam. She will never know how much her gesture means to me. She has no idea what to say, and that's exactly what she says. It is enough.

I do my best to keep my head up but feel eyes upon me constantly, real or imagined. Every day when I leave town, I drive past the red, four-story brick building where Katie was arrested: 250 Washington Street. I will never forget this address. There's only two routes off the peninsula, and the fastest is past the constant reminder of what my child's life has become.

Traffic! Why does traffic always come to a dead stop in front of this goddamn building? I torture myself with scenarios of what happened there and alternate those stories with memories of her as the sweet, loving person I know. I see someone walking out of the building and my heart begins to pound in my chest. If it's her, I will try to remember to put the car in park before leaping out of it. I see my girl everywhere yet find her nowhere. It's not her. It's never her.

Katie was always shy and a bit of a prude. She was the one who wouldn't get undressed in the changing room in front of anyone. When I carefully explained to her about the birds and the bees, she gazed very seriously at me and asked, "Did you and Daddy do that twice?" Sensing that even twice was more than she was interested in knowing about, I said, "Yes, honey, we wanted you and your brother." A look of utter disgust swept across her face and she stared me straight in the eye. Speechless for a moment, she gathered her composure: "We will never speak of this again."

It takes everything I have not to burst out laughing now just thinking about it.

Sometimes I stop and stare into the foyer of 250 Washington.

I force myself not to think about the things that happened in that building. Directing my anger toward every person who didn't reach out, because I can't allow myself to be angry with Katie, I alternate between feeling sure that everyone knows and is talking about us and trying to convince myself that no one cares.

Turning down a one-way street, I pass the House of the Seven Gables, where Nathaniel Hawthorne once lived. Hawthorne is all around this area. One of his distant ancestors was a judge during the Salem witch trials, and he felt ashamed about it, as did some other family members who preceded him and who changed their name from "Hathorne" to "Hawthorne." Hawthorne wrote one of the best-selling books of his time; he knew a thing or two about social stigma and ostracism.

On the way home, I stop in the local bookstore where I used to bring Katie and Liam in better times, as a treat after they got a good grade. I go to the section in the small store that holds the classics and grab a new copy of *The Scarlet Letter*. Out of the corner of my eye, I spot a woman I worked with when I was teaching in the town's middle school.

For a moment, I think of slipping away before she notices me, but before I am able to execute the turn she spots me, and I catch the recognition in her face. Does she see the woman she shared lunch and stories with for years or the mother of the girl who was arrested for selling herself for heroin?

"I wanted to call to see if you're okay," she says awkwardly.

I suppose she thinks that this is what I want to hear, and I'm sure it is the best she can do, certainly more than anyone else has done. But this confirms what I believe: that everyone in town is talking about us. What I wanted from her or any of the other people I had shared every day of my life with for the last few years—the people who coached Katie's softball games and whose children played alongside her, the families so grateful that she had been kind to their autistic children when they attended the summer camp where she volunteered, the friends and their parents she went to school and church alongside—was anything at all. I just wanted to hear anything from anyone.

"Why didn't you?" I ask.

She pauses, stunned. There is no good answer to my question. I break the silence.

"Don't worry, you're in good company. No one else said anything, either," I relate flatly, not caring about offending anyone. Let this story get out. Tell everyone you know how angry I am. Tell them how I didn't apologize or make excuses.

"No one?" she asks.

This is not entirely accurate: Mary Quinlan called, and days after the arrest news broke, Lisa, who I also used to work with, saw me stopped in traffic in front of the school where we once taught and said, "I'm thinking of you." That's all she said. So simple, all that was needed. Two people out of twenty thousand. Not a great statistic.

"If you don't know what to say," I tell my former colleague now, "then say, 'I don't know what to say, but I'm thinking of you.' I know it's uncomfortable, but say something."

She nods in agreement.

I remind myself never to let anyone off the hook for being silent because they are uncomfortable. Their uneasiness is not my problem. It is theirs.

And then, as if a long-imposed ban has been lifted, she begins to talk about addiction in her own family and tells me about a recent difficulty. It's not as extreme as Katie's case, but it's a real mess. I briefly wonder how many people are really commiserating rather than judging.

As the days pass, I become a shell of myself, walking like the dead through life, while my daughter injects herself with poison, slowly slipping away, occasionally texting to say that she loves me, sometimes sending unintelligible messages, just letters that have failed to coalesce into words. I know what she means, and tell her I love her more.

I'm told there is a saying that goes, "You are only as happy as your most unhappy child." As much as I don't want that to be true, I fear that it is. I wonder, much like I did as a child with my parents, *If she loves me, why won't she stop?* If she loves me and can't stop, maybe my parents loved me, too? An entire childhood of not letting anyone know the secret everyone knew. Years of protecting my children from ever being impacted by drugs or alcohol, and here we are. The opposite of everything I worked so hard to overcome. The irony is astounding. Will I ever be free of addiction?

Without thinking about where I am headed, I find myself at Chandler Hovey Park and walk out on the rocks below Marblehead Lighthouse. From here, I can gaze out over the entire town of Marblehead. To my right is Fort Sewall, the northeastern point of the main peninsula, on a promontory that overlooks the entrance to Marblehead Harbor, where the USS *Constitution* sought protection when Nathaniel Hawthorne was just a child and where the remnants of a stockade that held confederate soldiers are still standing. I imagine that Hawthorne stood in this place in the late 1840s, on one of his many long solitary walks, pondering his birthplace's puritanical past, inspired by the judgment and punishment inflicted toward anything not understood. I fear that Katie is now marked in a town where history never dies. Hawthorne said it perfectly:

She could no longer borrow from the future to help her through the present grief. . . . The days of the far-off future would toil onward, still with the same burden for her to take up and bear along with her, but never to fling down, for the accumulating days and added years would pile up their misery upon the heap of shame.

They think they can make a public spectacle out of my daughter. Having never quite fit in with the prominent, long-dwelling locals or new yuppie wannabes trying to keep up with one another, I suspect that Katie and I are now both pariahs. Let them talk. I know the truth. That is not Katie who was arrested, it's another person, afflicted with some sort of disease.

I contact that shitty, birdcage liner of a paper but never get a response. This secrecy and silence needs to end. I need to speak up.

I need to find the fearlessness that Katie found—although there's no telling how high she was when she apologized publicly on Facebook. I'm sure there have to be other people suffering in the same way. I don't even have a clue as to where to begin, but I know I need to find them in order to help Katie. I have never felt more alone.

This is a turning point in my life. I will look back on this day and realize that at that moment, there was no use trying to hide this from myself, or anyone else, for that matter. The cat was out of the bag, as they say. This is the moment when I grasped that there could be no going back, but that day at the lighthouse, I don't understand what that means or where it will lead. I do know that I will refuse to be quiet about this any longer. The silence is killing me, Katie, and so many more. Fuck this town! Fuck being quiet! Where do they think all of this started, if not in their own backyards?

three | Early Summer (Part One)

"Please go down the hall and see if you can make an appointment with Dezra Kenney and then another to see Dr. B in Beverly to talk," my therapist, Candace, implores. "I wish I could help you with Katie, but I think Dezra knows more than I do. Just do those two things. You don't even have to take the medication, just talk to Dr. B about it."

I've been seeing Candace for eight years now, and I trust her but don't always follow her advice, usually to my detriment. Candace has seen it all with me, although Katie's heroin addiction puts us in new territory and she worries about how I am holding up.

After our session is over and another appointment is made, as I promised, I take a right instead of the usual left at the elevator. I stand at Dezra Kenney's door and pause. Dr. Kenney is a psychiatrist who specializes in addiction. I have already done a little research and found out that her practice treats about two hundred people, mostly by prescribing medication-assisted treatments like Vivitrol, an opioid blocker, and Suboxone, which is a combination of an opioid and a blocker. She also does one-on-one and group counseling.

I expect to be taken back in time: rows of plastic bucket chairs bolted to the floor and to each other, posters on the walls about sharing needles, and dirty leftover hippies from the 1960s nodding out while waiting for their daily fix, looking higher when they leave than when they went in. I was a teenager when my grandmother went to a methadone clinic every day for a year to be weaned off the codeine she used to treat her migraines, whether she had a migraine or not. She didn't drive, so everyone took turns transporting her.

I have walked into the wrong office. This is a dental practice or the office of a chiropractor. I stand in line at the reception desk and look around. Several people sit in the waiting room: a young guy in a work uniform with "Tyler" written across the pocket; a young woman with long blond hair and a pudgy baby in a stroller; an older woman knitting. I wonder if Dr. Kenney shares space with another doctor.

The receptionist, who is trying to schedule someone on the phone, looks up with a smile, raising a finger to signify that she'll be right with me. I study the rack of brochures and flyers hanging on the wall. I take one of each. I have read everything I can online, but most of it says the same thing over and over and little of it feels like it applies to my situation. There's a blue-and-white brochure for a place called Learn to Cope that catches my eye. Its name rings familiar. Randy had sent me a link to the website, but I didn't investigate, still hoping that this would all pass quickly and there would be no need. *Learning to cope* sounds like both the exact thing I need to do and absolutely impossible. The organization is a nonprofit that holds meetings, meetings for parents and the loved ones of someone who is using opioids. I had been to Al-Anon meetings earlier in my life and hated them. I found them frustrating; the only thing I could ever think of, while watching the clock for the end of the meeting, was getting the hell out of there.

Just as I am about to escape without making an appointment, a woman on line behind me whispers, "Those meetings saved my sanity." She points to the days, times, and locations on the flyer posted on the wall.

"Oh, look, we have the same purse," she notes.

Mine is black, while hers is a deep chocolate brown color I prefer. Her hair is perfectly done, and she is wearing a smart work outfit. *Together* is how I'd describe her.

My bag was a gift, an "extravagant for me" Coach bag. I look down at myself and decide I am the farthest thing from together: no makeup, my hair pulled back in a ponytail, wearing an old T-shirt and the only shorts that fit me, even though they have a paint stain across the front that I choose to ignore. *Falling apart* is a more apt description for me.

I see that there's a local meeting at a Salem hospital on Thursdays. I write the information down and thank her, leaving with the brochure and without making an appointment. There is not enough air in the hallway; there is not enough air in the world to deal with the need to escape from this. The hope of addiction as a fleeting phase in Katie's life has passed, and the fact of this keeps hitting me in waves. The hope of Katie being somehow different from other people, exceptional, is fading. There are other people with not only the same purse but the same problem.

Spring evaporates into summer, and the letter box fills up with warrants and medical bills. Katie has not only been arrested for prostitution but also, twice, for possession of heroin around the same time. Summonses? They come in the mail, too. Hospital bills indicate that she has overdosed, and while they demand payment, the institution's personnel can neither confirm nor deny that she is or was a patient or why she has been treated, because of HIPAA privacy laws. My daughter's life is written up in great detail by bureaucrats and officers.

"Fuck you if you think I'm paying this," I scream at the innocent hospital billing clerk, who I've deemed guilty by association.

"Why do they keep releasing her?" I yell out to the empty house.

Each day I get a text, but little more.

"I ok lov u"

"Mis u"

"Mommy"

Mommy is the worst. Is she asking if I am there? Did she pass out in midsentence? Is this her last word? I imagine the next day telling the police, when they come to the door to inform me that she is gone, that she tried to contact me but all she could say was *Mommy* and it is all my fault for not responding, not knowing where she was, not helping her. What kind of mother doesn't know where her child is?

On the odd occasion when she calls, I at first sidestep around telling her to get help, then eventually beg her to go back to treatment.

"Katie, please, just let me see you" turns into "Just let me help you." This only causes her to stop calling and limit me to texts.

I drive around Salem, through areas where I think she might be, trying to find her. Past seedy motels, places known for drug use, and down streets I have heard her mention. I steer my car along Lynn Shore Drive, where she used to run miles on the walkway around the beach every day, what feels like just yesterday. Every young girl jogging could be her, but none are. I scan the newspapers each day for her name. I call the local hospitals in the middle of the night to see if my recurring nightmare that she needs me is real. A ladybug flies into my car, and I imagine it means something because that is my pet name for her. Always looking for signs of her.

I continue my slide into oblivion, being in a room while totally removed from everything going on around me. I forget what I am saying in the middle of sentences. I try to participate in life, but it is all an act, and I fool myself into believing that I am playing it well. I may look like I am making dinner or talking about the news, but I am either wondering what Katie is doing or trying to figure out what I can do to help her. I can't turn it off; it's like cable news in my head. I am not available to anyone, not even myself.

On an unseasonably cool Monday in July, I am happy to get into the car and make the twenty-minute drive to see Candace. I haven't left the house since Saturday and have barely spoken to anyone since Friday evening.

I drive down Route 1A in Lynn, hugging the coast, the skyline of Boston off in the distance, past the place where Katie jogged each morning before work and school. Candace has recently moved her office from Salem to her home and taken me with her.

"Okay, you win, I made the appointment with Dr. B," I say, sitting on her couch in the study filled with family pictures, books, and a piano. Dr. B. is the psychiatrist Candace suggested. I am careful to avoid the subject of Dezra Kenney, with whom I did not make an appointment.

"Well, I'm not sure that constitutes me winning anything, but I'm glad you are going."

Candace is visibly relieved. She's been suggesting this for a while, and I know she believes it will help me.

I once again give her all my reasons why I do not want to take medication, including the fact that I am appropriately depressed and medication isn't going to change that. I explain all this, wildly inflating my control of the situation. I am moving and taking action. That's not what a depressed person does. Secretly, I feel that medication is for weak people. Look at the havoc it's wreaked in my life! Getting on the drug bandwagon doesn't seem like a good choice.

"How was your weekend?"

She makes a good point. I have just spent the weekend alone, hiding in my house, so I entertain the idea that I may be wrong.

"The weekend was bad. Not just a little bad—'the reason I am keeping the appointment' bad."

Candace is not your usual therapist, the sort who doesn't give an opinion, thank God, but she still has moments when she sits quietly and waits for me to take the conversation where it needs to go.

"I can't find Katie. I keep looking, and the hospital bills keep coming in, and the warrants, and I think my older kids hate me, and maybe Randy is starting to hate me, too, and to be honest, I hate me more than anyone. I just want to stop this, go back to before it all started. I had no idea how lucky I was."

"How far back would you go?"

"I don't know. I don't know when it started. I still don't know what I could have done to change this. What thing I could have done better or not at all or how I could have fixed this. I just don't want this to be my life anymore. It just keeps coming at me in waves. I think it can't get any worse, and then it does."

"Maybe you can't fix it."

"I have to be able to fix it, don't you see that? If I can't fix it, who will?"

She is quiet, and I get the feeling I am supposed to figure this out, but I can't. I reach into my purse and check to see if Katie has texted me and then realize where I am and apologize.

"It's your time. You can use this session in any way you choose," Candace calmly says.

I'm not even sure what that means anymore.

I am in Dr. B's waiting room. I check my phone incessantly. E-mail to text message to Facebook Messenger and back again. Nothing. There is no one else here except a woman reading a magazine with her head turned and her hand shading her eyes. Engrossed in my own neurotic checking and rechecking of Katie's Facebook page, I don't notice at first that the woman is a teacher from the middle school where I taught, someone I always thought was so together. She finally looks up, possibly realizing there is no way to avoid a conversation, and we chat briefly, with a total lack of acknowledgment that we are both in a psychiatrist's office.

Finally, I am called in. There's no couch to lie on, so I take a seat in the chair across the room. Dr. B sits at her desk and asks a series of questions about my overall health. She is dressed simply, and the room is sparsely furnished and barely decorated, as if she has just moved in or, possibly, is just moving out.

"Any thoughts of harming yourself?"

"No."

"Any thoughts of harming others?"

"Is that wrong?"

The joke falls flat. Maybe because I'm not sure I'm joking. I think about Chad and Gabe Wright. There's a gap between wanting to hurt someone and actually doing it, isn't there?

"I'm kidding, of course. I'm in great health, and I don't want to hurt anyone. This isn't even my idea; it's my therapist's. I keep telling her I'm fine. Anyone would be depressed in my situation. I really didn't want medication, but I promised I'd speak with you."

The doctor explains that my reasoning is flawed.

"Yes," she agrees, "you have every reason to be depressed, and a pill isn't going to fix your situation. But what you are experiencing in your life—the lack of concentration, the getting lost driving a route you've been down a thousand times, the inability to participate in a conversation or finish a sentence, the circular, repeating thoughts— that's anxiety. A small dose of Zoloft would be worth trying," she explains. "You can stop if it doesn't help, and you can cut the pill in half to start."

I leave with the prescription and even fill it, fully intending to never take it.

The following Monday morning comes, and I'm a wreck. Not six months have elapsed since I found my jewelry missing, but it feels like a lifetime. Katie has agreed to meet me at Red's at nine a.m. for breakfast, and I promise myself that I will not fight or talk about drugs or treatment. I vow to filter everything I say through the knowledge that one wrong word could send her away from me again. I fantasize that she'll show up with a suitcase, asking me to take her to detox.

Red's Sandwich Shop occupies the ground floor of a well-known three-story, pitched-roof red wooden house dating back to 1698. Though the restaurant now doles out breakfast and lunch to tourists and locals, the premises were the original site of the Old London Coffee House, the gathering place of patriots before the American Revolution. Beside the huge fireplace, men argued about unfair British taxes. The building was once home to the Salem Fraternity, the oldest boys' club in America. I'm sure no one would have ever thought that in 2015 it would be known for the size of its giant pancakes.

———

see Katie walking toward me without all her belongings—without any—and I'm mildly disappointed. Then she spots me and gives me a huge smile, and my heart fills with love. For just a minute, she's my sweet girl. She begins to run, then skip toward me like she did when she was little. It's well over eighty degrees, though, and she is wearing long sleeves. She rushes me, and we hug in the middle of the street. I can feel the bones of her rib cage around her back. She's a petite girl, but she feels like a child. She smells of cigarettes and something else I can't place. Her long hair, dyed black, is pulled back in a clip, and she is uncharacteristically without makeup. Her eyebrows, by her own admission, need to be plucked and shaped, something she had always been very careful about. And her eyes look blank and dull, her pupils pinned in the sun. She's high. She looks worn out behind the smile. As much as I want to, I am careful not to remark on that—or anything else related to it. Instead, I hold on to her for as long as she will let me, feeling like a bird has landed on my fingertip and afraid that it will fly away.

We have breakfast and talk around anything of importance. She eats as if she hasn't eaten in a month. She tells me to listen to the new Imagine Dragons song "I Bet My Life," because it reminds her of us. I pay little attention because I'm consumed with how she keeps nodding off and the impossibility that she believes I can't tell just how fucked up she is in front of me.

When I ask her where she is living, she avoids the question, so I remind myself not to ask it again.

Anything I say or do might send her away. I feel so close to her agreeing to come home with me, to get clean, to do the right thing. I color my conversation with all the positive, happy things going on in my life. In other words, I lie like a rug. She fades in and out and talks of nothing; I study her while she eats. The check comes, and I realize that she is neither coming home nor going to treatment. I hadn't prepared to let her go.

I offer to give her a ride, thinking I may be able to figure out where she is staying. She declines. She needs to meet a friend. Standing next to my car, she gives me another hug, thanking me and telling me she loves me as she walks down the one-way street in the opposite direction of traffic. There's no way to follow her, so I watch her turn the corner and then sit on the curb. I'm not sure how long I stare at the place where she disappeared, but eventually I gather myself together and begin to drive around again, looking for her.

Randy and I haven't seen each other in over a week and have barely spoken. I'm trying to be the person he wants me to be, but I'm baffled that he can't see that I need to be constantly available. The fact that doing so is killing me isn't important. I convince myself that if he were in the same situation, he would be doing the same thing, although I honestly don't believe that. The fight is always the same. I apologize and then become more careful, and resentful, about not being able to check my phone while he is in the room. He doesn't understand, I tell myself, and I imagine that the other parents who are dealing with this, who aren't as screwed up as their kids, are as vigilant as I am.

Of course, I don't know anyone going through this, so I'm not sure, but I tell myself this is true.

The phone rings three times before Randy answers; he is on his way to work, and he's surprised to hear from me. I struggle to sound upbeat and make some small talk, ask about his son and their weekend.

"I found a meeting in Salem," I tell him. "It's for parents who have a child who is addicted to heroin. You sent me a link for the website a few months ago."

"Have you gone?"

"Well, no, not yet."

To fill the ensuing silence, I add, "I also went to the psychiatrist, and she gave me a prescription for something to help with the anxiety."

"Have you taken it?" he asks.

"I'll go to the meeting. I promise."

"I don't think you understand what it's like to be with you," he says. "It's like you're not even in the room with me. I'm dating a ghost."

Something about that strikes a chord and sits with me. It's exactly how I feel. I'm not anywhere that I physically am. I'm lost in thought and obsessed with Katie, guilty over not being there for my other children, worried about the work that I can't concentrate long enough to do, afraid of losing the man I love, and painfully and deeply lonely and lost.

I quietly make the decision to start the medication and tell no one. I dig out the Learn to Cope pamphlet.

Looking up the group online, I find the meeting schedule. The next meeting is Thursday—tonight—and I'm free and without a conflict that could prevent me from attending. I tell Randy I'm going in an e-mail, and he calls me later that afternoon.

"I changed my mind," I say.

"Why?" he asks. I can hear the resignation in his voice.

"I'm not going to talk, and it's just going to be a few people I have nothing in common with sitting around complaining. I think it would be better for me if I just took a long walk. It's such a beautiful night."

"Go to the meeting. You can take a walk any night. Go to the meeting."

He isn't the only one who has had enough. I am tired of walking around waiting for the aftershock of the bomb blast. I open the lockbox hidden in my office closet—that's where I keep any medication now—and pull out the bottle of Zoloft. I had convinced myself that I still had everything under control because I wasn't taking medication every day. I still had a choice. For me at this moment, taking a pill every day symbolizes finally giving up on myself and my ability to remain strong; it means admitting that I can't handle it all, that I need help. It feels like defeat.

I extract a small blue, oval-shaped pill and go to the kitchen and cut it in half, as the doctor suggested doing at first. Grabbing a water bottle, I sit on the floor with my back against the fridge and put my head back to stare at the ceiling.

"Please, God, please make this all stop. I know I can't handle one more thing, and seriously, I don't ask for much. And, Mom, if you're up there, too, please take care of my baby. I'm thinking you owe me one."

Letting down my last defenses, I pop the blue half of a pill into my mouth and swallow.

"Okay, now I'm officially broken," I say to no one and get up and wait to see what happens.

I close my eyes and open them again. "Nope, not fixed yet!"

I'm not sure whether it is because Randy is right or because there was an implied ultimatum, but I decide to go to the meeting. Only there's a catch: if I have to go, then someone else has to come with me.

"Remember the meeting where you get the free Narcan? Well, it's tonight at six."

"Thanks for the warning," says Mike. A while back, he'd mentioned that he wanted to have an antidote for overdoses on hand. "Are you going?"

"Yes, and you need to go, too. She's not just my daughter."

"Don't get your knickers in a twist. I didn't say I wouldn't go. I have something I want you to give Katie anyhow. I'll meet you there."

I'm attacking him, and I'm not even sure why.

Pulling into the parking lot shortly before the start of the six-thirty p.m. meeting—I gave Mike an earlier time because he tends to run late—I check the room and entrance number several times and remind myself why I am there: *Narcan* and *To be able to say I went*. The large meeting room is filled with fifty to sixty people sitting in concentric rows, in a large circle. Coffee and cookies are on a long table near the doorway; some even look misshapen, homemade. The walls are bare except for a large screen covering one side. A room full of accountants and customer service representatives and paralegals. One man in the back is laughing loudly, his phone in a heavy plastic case strapped to his belt; a contractor, definitely, I decide. I must be in the wrong place again, I think, and am on my way back out the door when a woman introduces herself.

"Hi, I'm Kathy. Are you looking for the Learn to Cope meeting?" she asks.

"Yes, I am," I answer with a laugh, waiting for her to tell me where that meeting is.

"Welcome," she says. She is warm and friendly, the sort of person who exudes kindness with just a hello. It takes me a moment to realize that I am where I intended to be.

"Is this your first meeting?" she asks. "I conduct a Narcan training session for anyone who's new, and if you'd like to come with me, it will take about fifteen minutes, and then you can rejoin the meeting. You won't miss much, and we have a really good speaker tonight."

At that point, I would have followed her to a human sacrifice. The relief of being out of that room—full of people who look exactly like me, seemingly intelligent, engaged, and appearing more like participants in a PTA meeting than a group of people whose children are addicted to heroin—is overwhelming.

But when Kathy begins her tutorial for myself and several others, the idea of assembling a dose of Narcan, or remembering anything she says to me, in the midst of finding my child overdosed and near death strikes me as improbable at best. She explains that this drug will reverse the effects of the opioid, which in too large a hit shuts down the respiratory system, causing death. Kathy gives an efficient demonstration of how to do rescue breathing, after calling 911, and then how to administer a second dose if the first one doesn't work. I am told to keep breathing for Katie while I wait for the ambulance. I wonder how to do that when it's doubtful, given that situation, that I'd remember to breathe myself.

I'm being shown how to save my child's life in a room full of people who also need this information. How the fuck did I get here?

Mike arrives late, even though I told him the meeting started thirty minutes before it actually began, but when I return after the training, he is sitting in the group. No leaving now, I suppose. When he sees me, an expression of relief floods his face, and he pats the seat next to him. The poor guy is sweating, tapping his leg up and down, and looks about as close to a stroke as I've ever seen him. He is holding a medium-sized white plastic bag, and as soon as I sit down, he tries to show me something inside it. Mike keeps trying to tell me what is in the bag, but I can't hear him over the crinkling. The crinkling of the bag sounds magnified, it's the world's loudest fucking bag, and he won't stop crinkling it; it's louder than the leader of the group, who has begun the meeting. The group leader has a microphone, for Christ's sake, and all I can hear is the bag. I reach over and hold the bag still and give Mike what my kids fondly call the Look of Death. He stops.

Dear God, help me from killing him, I silently pray.

The speaker is a man my age who has been sober for over twenty-five years. Sean-Michael explains in his heavy South Boston accent that he is making a documentary and is looking for families to participate. Mike and I both gape at each other as if this man has lost his mind. When I glance back at the room, dumbfounded, hands are raised, all sorts of people volunteering. Are they insane? Do they understand how they will feel when everyone knows? Maybe the newspaper hasn't published a story on their child. Sean-Michael assures everyone that he will speak to them after the meeting and launches into his story.

He tells a tale of heroin use, jail, and more heroin. His only sobriety was in prison, and even then, he managed to find drugs. His mother was his one constant source of support. She never gave up on him, never denied him a hot meal. Loved him unconditionally. Always put him ahead of herself and never held a grudge, no matter what he stole from her, including her peace. His mother was a good Irish mother, he told us, and she thought he walked on water, no matter what he did.

Vindicated, I looked at Mike. *Yes, I am that kind of mother.*

"I had been missing for a few weeks," he went on. "Recently out of jail again, and she had taken me in. She convinced her brother to hire me, and I immediately stole and sold some copper off a job site and disappeared, staying barely alive in a crack house nearby, until the money and drugs ran out. My plan was that I'd go home, take a shower and eat a home-cooked meal, and then with her help figure out my next step."

The room is silent. The parents are all waiting for the answer we want to hear. I am sure that he's about to explain that this was the moment, over a warm bowl of soup, when he came to his mother and told her he was done. She had loved him enough for him to quit using drugs.

"I got to the door," he says, "and she saw me coming up the walk and she opened the door. *Thank God for mothers*, I thought. Then she did something she had never done before. Instead of widening the door and welcoming me in, she stepped onto the porch and Bridget O'Leary put her foot down and said 'Get off my property, Sean-Michael, and don't come back until you are done using drugs for good. I love you with all of my heart, and if you die I will mourn you every day until I join you, but I am not going down this road with you anymore. You need to help yourself, and until you are ready to do that, don't come back.'"

Several people wipe their eyes. Others nod their heads in agreement. I believe my mouth is open in shock. The realization that his mother had done that to him and he was still sitting in front of me took me aback.

"I'll never forget that moment," he says. "God rest her soul. She took control, and the one person that would always be there for me was gone. I turned, and for the next few weeks I continued on the run I had started at sixteen. Then one morning I woke up and realized that life was going on with or without me. I was sick and tired of being sick and tired. I had lost everything, and the pain of getting sober was finally not as bad as the pain of trying to stay high. I entered a program for what seemed like the hundredth time and the first time as well. Something had changed, and I can't tell you whether it was my mother or if I had just had enough, but I was done. That's not to say that it's not still difficult at times, but that was the last time I used. I slowly built a new relationship with my family and took my life back. My mother never saw me high again, and she lived another twenty years. I was the one everyone counted for dead, and I came back. Don't ever lose hope."

The meeting ends with the group standing, everyone holding hands, and reciting the Serenity Prayer:

> "God, grant me the serenity to accept the things I
>   cannot change,
> The courage to change the things I can,
> And the wisdom to know the difference."

"Keep coming back," they all say in unison.

Mike is a heartbroken wreck and, still holding the noisy bag, heads home. It's a relief not to have to watch him suffering. I sit back down and I am paralyzed. *Now what?*

"Hi, I'm Marion," says the woman next to me. She lightly puts an arm around my shoulders and asks, "Do you need a hug?"

Just a few words, and they hit me harder than when Martin found me in the blizzard and asked if I needed help. I turn to Marion and burst into tears. I haven't allowed myself to cry because I'm not sure if I'll ever stop, and now that I've started, in public of all places, I realize that I may be right.

I can feel the energy of the room dissipating, and the voices that had filled it are now moving toward the hallway. Marion says nothing at first and sits with me while I sob. There's nothing to say, and she knows that; she is in the same place. A few miles away, a boy rather than a girl, not quite the same age—but as we begin to talk, I can hear that all the pieces of the story that are important are the same.

She asks me a bit about Katie and talks for a while about her son, Brian. Marion and Brian are both sports fanatics: baseball, football, and especially basketball. She adores him—you can see it in her eyes. He's doing well right now, but it's been a long, hard road and she is far from relaxed.

"How long have you been dealing with this?" I ask.

"Oh, it's going on four years," she replies.

I'm stunned. She's still hopeful after four years.

"How do you keep going?" I blubber. "Why won't they stop?"

"Relapse is very often part of this disease," Marion explains. "You have to get yourself connected to other people and educate yourself. That's the only way to get through this. These meetings are a good start, but if you're quiet, like I am, you'll do better online. Have you heard of the Addict's Mom, Wicked Sober, and Mike Duggan or Matt Ganem?"

I shake my head no and start to cry again. I have obviously missed something important by hiding in my house.

"You do have a Facebook account, right?"

"Yes, yes, I do."

I have heard of none of these people or groups. I had been searching online for things I could do or say, for places to send Katie, and hunting through news articles for her name, but it had never occurred to me to look on Facebook for an answer. Marion gives me her number and makes me promise not only to come back to Learn to Cope but also to call her if I need anything. Then she writes down the names of the groups I should join on Facebook and how to reach out to Matt "the Poet" Ganem.

"He will help you," she assures me.

With no idea how a poet or a Facebook group might possibly help me, I promise I will do as she has told me to do. I leave feeling slightly less alone and a little more educated.

I step out into the warm July night air and head home. There, I sign in to Facebook. There is a one-sentence message from Katie:

"Mommy I don't want to do this anymore."

I read it a hundred times. I message her back. I tell her I'm here, that I love her, that I'll come get her—all with no reply. I imagine again that those are her last words, and I call all the local hospitals to see if she is there. I join groups and send friend requests to strangers, one of them Marion, another Matt the Poet. I read other people's stories and about their heartbreak, and I know I won't sleep tonight. At three a.m., Katie still hasn't checked her messages and I am still searching for information when she posts a picture of herself and three friends at Foxwoods casino in Connecticut. They all look happily fucked up.

I put the computer and the phone away for the first time in almost twenty-four hours and try to sleep for a little while before I have to go to work. I remind myself of the words of Bridget O'Leary's son, Sean-Michael, from what seems like light-years before but was only this past evening.

Never give up hope.

four | # Late Summer (Part Two)

The steamy heat of August that everyone is complaining about is the least of my problems. It has been almost two and half months since Katie's first arrest and over a month since I met her for breakfast. Two more warrants come to the house, both for possession of heroin: one occurred nearby, in Salem, after she was pulled over in a 2015 red Chevy pickup truck, the other in a town I didn't know she had ever been to, over an hour away. I search my mind for who might have enough money to own a red truck or who she might know in Lowell. I once shared everything with my child; I now know nothing of her life. Everywhere I go, I think I see her.

Every day I pass 250 Washington Street, the run-down brick building where she was arrested, and if a group of people are outside, my heart all but stops. A small park is across the street. It is evident that drugs are plentiful there, by the look of the people, old and young, sitting on benches, lying on the ground, and nodding off while standing up. How many times have I driven past this park and not seen what is so obvious now?

It's been four days without any contact, with no posts on Face-book, and she has not checked Messenger. I'm driving to an insurance client, trying to carry out the tasks I need to go on with to pay my bills. Stopped at the light in front of 250 Washington, I turn my head toward the park and I see her. Even from the car I can tell she is high because of the way she is stooped over, leaning on a bench. Her hair is pulled up in a bandanna I've never seen before, and she's wearing a light green dress that shows the sharpness of her thin shoulders. She is smoking a cigarette, which, for some reason, even after all of this, makes me mad.

The light turns green and I pull over, half-parking, the rear of the vehicle jutting out into traffic. I jump out of the car, forgetting to turn off the engine. I run through the park calling her name, attracting little attention in a place where people are numb to a commotion. The small child she is with turns first, but she doesn't seem to hear me and turns toward me only as I am almost touching her, shocking us both.

The woman who faces me looks to be about my age, and braces herself for what appears to be an attack. She moves toward the child on the ground, quickly picking him up, and throws her cigarette onto the dirt. She's worn and hard-looking, barely ninety pounds, and is missing several teeth on the right front side of her mouth, caving in her face significantly on that side.

"I'm so sorry. Oh, my God, I'm sorry I scared you. I thought you were my daughter."

I hear horns and a traffic jam behind me and glance backward to see the congestion I've caused with my car, more in the street than on the shoulder.

"You thought I was your daughter?" she asks, as though it is the most blatant lie she has ever heard in a life that has involved more than her fair share.

"I can't find her. I'm sorry. Everyone looks like her lately."

My voice is cracking, and I choke back tears and apologize again as I start to walk away.

"I hope you find her, honey," the woman who is not my daughter calls.

I raise my hand up but don't turn around, afraid that from a distance she will look like Katie again—or what Katie may look like someday.

Searching the *Salem News* for Katie's name is the first thing I do with my morning coffee, but in early August, the name that shows up in the news is not Kaitlin Harvey's but Dezra Kenney's. The recovery advocate, addiction specialist, and therapist has died suddenly; there is no mention of a cause of death. My heart breaks for all the people who depend on her, for her staff and her family, and for my own slow, loosening hold on hope.

Finally, Katie surfaces, calling her father for a ride and swearing she'll go to treatment at a hospital in New Hampshire. Too elated to question why it has to be a hospital in New Hampshire and armed with our good insurance, Mike drives to meet Katie in New Hampshire. He is horrified at what he finds. Katie was already thinner than she should be, but now she's twenty pounds lighter. Her hands are filthy, and there is dirt under her nails. He almost doesn't recognize her. Her face is scabbed and picked, and the scent of her is so foul that he rides with the windows open. She smells of cigarettes and dirty laundry and withdrawal. Shoeless, she has nothing but a shopping bag, everything she owned gone again. After nodding off in the car, her body periodically shaken by small tremors, she vomits up the lunch her father forced on her.

When they get to the out-of-network hospital in New Hampshire, our insurer refuses to cover the inpatient rate. With a doctor who has never seen her claiming her treatment is not medically necessary, hospital personnel refer her to their outpatient clinic, which will open again in three days.

And then, she is gone again.

Hope without knowledge is worthless. That is what I have learned throughout my life. I've always believed that if one other person can accomplish a goal, then with enough determination and education, so can I. So now, I set out to absorb all I can.

I learn other people's stories, and almost as quickly, I see how remarkably similar they are. A son's football injury, a prescription for pain meds, and one day he overdoses on heroin and is revived by Narcan outside a movie theater. His parents had no idea. A wife's drinking problem seems to get worse, the joint checking account heads south, a child asks, "What's wrong with Mommy?" They catch it early. A man—a brother, a son, and a husband—is found in a park, an overdose. He dies on the way to the hospital. He had been sober for just shy of a year.

I go to events. Having heard Dr. Ruth Potee speak at one, I introduce myself and tell her about my nonprofit, trying to see how the mission of Magnolia New Beginnings might dovetail with the growing need for community and information. Dr. Potee has the ability to explain complex subjects in a way that is understandable.

"Just as diabetes is caused by a broken insulin receptor, addiction is caused by broken dopamine receptors or other parts of the brain's internal pleasure center," she says. "I think of it as a broken brain. Like a broken leg, it gets better. But it takes a long time. The days of us thinking of this"—addiction—"as a moral weakness or a failing or bad parenting or bad genetics—we've got to move past that."

I learn about how drugs affect the prefrontal cortex and the reward center of the brain, the nucleus accumbens. "This critical part of the brain is the reward center," Dr. Potee goes on. "It's the part of the brain that tells you you've done a good job: you got up, you found food, you found water." Dr. Potee says dopamine is a chemical that's released when a person does something that their brain judges to be beneficial, and the release makes them feel good. "But drugs cause unnaturally high spikes in dopamine," she explains, "which causes the brain to adjust to produce less dopamine, and drug users eventually continue their use just to feel normal again, because their baseline level of dopamine has become very low."

Until about the age of twenty-four, when the brain is fully formed, genetics play a major role in terms of whether a person becomes addicted. I never understood why it wasn't me. How in the world, with the trauma and constant substance abuse I was surrounded by, could I not have had a problem myself? Now I began to understand. There was a time when I believed I was smarter and stronger than anyone in my family. After learning more about addiction, I quickly came to realize that I was just luckier. In this game of Russian Roulette: Genetics Edition, I got the empty chamber. Katie, on the other hand, had been given a fully loaded gun.

It all starts to make sense. I had been so sure that setting a good example, loving my children, and not allowing them to experience the trauma associated with drugs and domestic violence would be enough. My goal was to raise my children the exact opposite way of how I grew up. I had hoped nurture could overrule nature, without understanding the disease model of addiction and genetics.

Much to my surprise, the Zoloft starts to work. Not in enormous ways, but in ways that only I and possibly Randy notice. I haven't told him yet, but we are getting along better, and I want to share this news with him. We are in his yard, cleaning up branches after a storm, some days after I moved from only half a pill to the full 50 milligrams once a day, and I am feeling a little floaty.

"If I seem a little off," I confide, "it's because I started taking the prescription that the psychiatrist gave me. I don't know if you noticed."

He stops in his tracks, branch in hand, and looks down first, then straight at me. "Yes, I noticed. I didn't know what it was, but it's amazing. You're like a different person. No, you're like *you* again."

That makes me happy and sad at the same time. I need a pill to be myself? The irony is not lost. I don't want that, but I also know that I am not getting lost in my head the way I had been, and that is a great relief.

The next morning, Randy and I take separate cars to an outdoor addiction awareness event in New Hampshire. He comes for moral support—and to make sure I actually go, I'm sure. He brings his son with him, and afterward they head up to the White Mountains for a hike. This is my official coming-out party. My first public event.

Marion had reached out and told me that she would be attending and that Matt Ganem would also be; I really wanted to meet him in person. Still angry at how no one had reached out to me when Katie was arrested, I wear my Marblehead T-shirt, hoping there will be press and I can get in a picture. If the town is going to "out" my daughter, I am going to "out" the town.

Banyan Treatment Center, where Matt works in community outreach, wants to send a busload of people to attend the Fed Up! Rally and the Unite to Face Addiction concert in Washington, D.C., at the beginning of October, and the planning for that meant a nonprofit would have to receive the donation of the money to pay for the bus. I volunteered to do it through Magnolia. I resurrected and refiled the paperwork I had let lapse, and Magnolia has been reenergized!

Something good will come out of all this heartbreak. This hell I am going through won't be for nothing.

"That's Matt," Marion leans over and tells me.

Matt spots Marion, and his face lights up. He is the sweet boy I've been relying on recently to tell me what to say and what not to say to Katie when she contacts me, which has been sporadic and brief. I have spoken and texted with him so often I feel like I already know him.

As he greets Marion with a warm hug, it is apparent that they have genuine affection for each other. Matt's been in recovery from drug addiction for years and has devoted himself to helping other people get into treatment. He will help anyone who comes to him, whether they want to go to his place of work or not. I'm told that this is unusual. I watch as he unpacks a box of books and places them on the far side of his table.

"Hi, Matt, I'm Maureen," I say. I, too, am greeted with a warm hug.

"It's so good to meet you in person," Matt says. "I can't believe you're not coming to Washington with us after you helped make the bus happen! It's going to be such an incredible trip."

Matt is surprisingly baby-faced, yet covered almost completely in tattoos. He looks like the sort of thug who might rob you and then apologize for it. He makes a point of listening with complete focus, so that when you're talking to him, you feel like, at that moment, you are the most important person in the room.

"I wish I could," I tell him, "but I'm just so swamped, and I can't leave right now."

Matt has been my port in the storm. When Katie texts me, saying how she can't do this anymore, I no longer trust that I'll say the right thing. Instead I forward the texts to Matt, and he tells me how to respond. He is my Cyrano; I cut and paste Katie's cries for help and send them to him, and he replies for me so that I can paste his words into a message back to Katie, giving her the perfect response.

"When are you going to let me adopt you?" I ask.

"I promise, I'll think about it," he answers with a laugh. "Call me if you need anything, and take Mike Duggan's number, too. He runs Wicked Sober, where I worked before Banyan. He's a good guy," Matt adds.

I believe him. At this point, I'd believe him if he told me fish could fly. I need to believe in someone. The more information and contacts, the better. I take the number and thank him for the hundredth time.

I still have the address in Quincy that Steven had provided when I'd grilled him after he'd driven Katie away on her first escape, from the sober living facility in Portland. After pouring over hundreds of numbers in my cell-phone records, which include a phone for Katie, I find a landline that corresponds to that address and increased recent activity to that phone. The FBI should hire mothers of children who are addicted to heroin, I think to myself. The homeowner's name is Jason, and I imagine a pimp and drug dealer but I don't care. I am too scared of losing Katie to be afraid of him.

On one of my Facebook parents' groups, a woman named Rhonda had mentioned "sectioning" her daughter. Section 35, I discover, is the civil commitment law in Massachusetts: if you fill out a ton of paperwork that proves a person is a harm to himself or others due to drugs or alcohol, a judge can issue a warrant for the police to pick him up. If the judge then grants the section, the person is taken to detox. The one caveat is that you need to know exactly where the person is, so that the police can retrieve him. If Mike and I can prove that Katie is a danger to herself or others, because of her drug addiction, she will be held in a special section of the state correctional facility, in a locked ward, and given some form of treatment. Our hope is that she will be confined long enough to see that she wants to get well. Anything is better than the street and the uncertainty, we finally conclude. Where once we debated which college would be better, now we vacillate between jail and the street.

Mike and I are two middle-aged, middle-class people driving through drug-infested neighborhoods, as determined to find Katie as she is desperate not to be found. Every person looks like her, and then turns out not to be her. It is a little past ten p.m. when I reach out to a woman I have never spoken to before, having only seen her posts on a Facebook group page, for suggestions on what to do if we find Katie. Rhonda explains exactly what I would need to say the following day in court to obtain a Section 35. The most important thing is being able to give the police an address.

I pray that when we find Katie, she can be talked into going to treatment. I imagine her seeing us and realizing how much we love her. I picture her running into my arms, happy to be found, and ready to get well.

When we're stopped at a light, the car in front of us rolls down a window. A young woman in a hoodie, with the hood pulled up over her head, approaches the car, leans in, and then quickly walks back to the group of people she had been standing with.

"Slow down, is that her?" I'm sure I see Katie crossing the street.

"Do you have your contacts in?"

"Yes, pull over! We're going to miss her."

"Are you feckin' blind? You do see that this girl is black, and unless Katie is now black, it's not her."

"Fuck off," I say.

We both have to laugh.

Rows of identical apartment buildings line the main street, filled with people living what they believe to be their own unique versions of life, most likely not that different from the neighbors with whom they share a wall. It is a warm night, and people are gathered outside in the front of one building, passing a bottle around and smoking. I picture my little girl among them. We find a parking spot nearby, and I force myself to get out of the car. As my feet crunch on broken glass, one of the younger men glances at us.

Slurring, a large, older man speaks to two younger men:

"Those tits were like beach balls. No, goddamn watermelons."

"How much?" asks the smaller, skinnier counterpart.

"Fifty an hour. But trust me, Little Man, you won't last an hour with Sheila."

I thank God it is not Katie they are talking about and say a silent prayer for Sheila and her mother. Mike and I exchange the same worn look.

The men look us over carefully, surely sensing that we do not belong, as we walk toward the high-rise building. I hear them laughing at us, or perhaps at Sheila, as we climb the front steps. I glance over at Mike and see our lives together flash before my eyes. We have known each other since our early twenties and have been through so much, but this is beyond anything we could have ever anticipated.

"You take me to all the nicest places," I say.

He is looking for his baby girl in a crack house, and despair is written across his face.

"Don't be mad at me, but if she's in there, she's coming with us," I announce.

"What do you mean?" he asks.

"I'm grabbing her and she's coming with us, even if I have to knock her unconscious. I am not leaving here without her."

"Oh, really? You are assuming you're going to get in. You have no idea what you're walking into—you think they're just going to open the door to you with a plate of cookies and welcome you in. You won't even get past the front door."

"Watch me," I say.

On the wall, there is a long panel of names and numbers next to buttons. There are no cameras. Without giving it too much thought, and to avoid backing out, I push the buzzer for 5D twice. Mike looks at me like I'm the world's biggest moron and starts to open his mouth. I shush him.

A man's voice croaks, "Hello."

"Hey, it's me," I say, my voice rising.

After a short delay, I hear the buzzer, pull the door, and we are in. I shoot a look over my shoulder and playfully give Mike the finger. Then I raise my arms, Rocky-like.

"I am clearly the brains of the operation."

"We are fucked if you're the brains," he says.

"You're not hitting anyone, understand?" I remind him. "We want information, and we can't get that if you start smacking people."

"It depends how hard I hit them. You'd be surprised how talkative these fuckers become with a good smack to the head."

The lights are out in the first-floor hallway, but I can see the paint peeling off the ceiling around the fixtures. The building is old, musty, and clearly uncared for. Televisions play behind the doors, a family is fighting in Spanish, the smell of cigarettes is in the air. We find the elevator and take it to the fifth floor.

"What's your plan now, Inspector Gadget?"

"I'm going to walk in the door and get my daughter. You should stay behind. I'm harmless, you're intimidating. As well as annoying."

"You're not going in there yourself, ya eejit."

The hallway is oddly silent, but I can hear the news from the door at 5A telling me that another hot day is on the way. Don Orsillo gives the play-by-play of the extra-innings Red Sox game behind the door of 5B. Mike slows to listen for the score: *It's 3–3 in the bottom of the tenth.* I stop and look at him, holding my hands out in front of me, questioning his sanity.

"Well, then come in, too," I say to him as I rap on the door of 5D, quickly moving out of the way of the peephole.

The door opens too slowly, and I prepare for there to be someone behind it. The idea that this person will have a gun pops into my head, but it's too late to do anything about it. The door eerily continues to creep open. The room is nearly empty except for a hospital bed in the far-right corner. I walk in and signal to Mike to stay behind. He doesn't listen and follows me in. The smell of burnt plastic takes me back to 1980s New York.

In the corner is Jason. The Jason I had pictured—angry, armed, and menacing—is nowhere to be found. In his place is a man in his thirties with little use of his arms and no legs, completely bedridden, who had opened the door with a button from his bed. He looks like an incapacitated Bilbo Baggins. The collection of leads, tubes, and bags attached to him made me think of some crazy science experiment.

There is nothing on the walls except for a whiteboard within sight distance of the bed with names and dates listed on it, much like you'd see in a hospital room. Out of the corner of my eye, beyond the small galley kitchen littered with empty liter bottles and medical supplies, I see Mike heading toward me while shaking his head, carrying some plastic bags I recognize as Katie's.

"They come here, her and Chad." Jason draws a long, shaky breath. "I keep telling her she needs to go home, get clean. I had hoped she did, because I haven't heard from her in a couple of weeks. She's not going to last on the street."

I want to hate him, but he is suffering in a way that is beyond anything I can understand, and really, I just want to get the hell out of that room.

"What now?" Mike asks me when we're in the elevator.

"I don't have a clue, but I'll think of something."

On the long, quiet, ride home, it comes to me. The red truck. The warrant from her arrest in Salem had a license plate number. If I can find out who owns the truck, I can find out if that person knows where Katie is staying.

Once again, I know people who can run a license plate for me. It's quite illegal, but these people don't care much about that, and for that I am grateful.

The following morning, I dig out Tony's phone number. Tony is as wide as he is tall, a perfect ball, and almost a parody of a shady used-car dealer. Every time I've gone into his dealership, there has always been food around and someone counting money in the back office, and Tony would always try to get me to have a little whiskey with him. He claims it will relax me. I feel that being tense in that place is appropriate.

"Tony, hey, how are you?"

"Maureen!" he bellows.

"Well, Tony, I've been better. My daughter is in trouble, and I need a favor."

"Okay, love, what do we have to do? Did someone hurt her? Anything you need."

Thoughts of people I'd like to knock off flood my mind.

"No, it's nothing like that. She's doing drugs, heroin, and I need to find her to get her into treatment. I have a plate number. I just need someone to run it so I can get an address."

"Done," Tony says. "Give it to me."

I recite the plate number, and Tony disappears without a word. Several minutes later he comes back on the phone with a full name I recognize and an address in Chelmsford.

"Where the hell is Chelmsford?" I ask.

"Near Lowell and Lawrence," he replies. "Lots of drugs out there. You let me know if you need anything else. Anything. Next time you're in this area, you stop by for a whiskey. It will relax you."

Somehow, the idea of being too relaxed with Tony while drinking makes me think I'd wake up the next morning in a cold bathtub, missing a kidney.

"I'll do that, Tony. Thank you. You're the best."

I text Mike saying I have an address in Chelmsford where she might be.

"How the hell did you get that?" he asks.

"I have friends in low places."

"Give it to me," he demands.

"Listen, you maniac, the idea is to find out exactly where she is and then have her sectioned. Rhonda gave me all the information on how to do it. The apartment belongs to a guy she was in treatment with—I recognize the name because I spoke to his wife. Remember? She was the one who came in with the newborn to visit him. I have a feeling that that's where she's staying. No one has seen her in weeks, or Chad. Not since they got arrested in that red truck, which belongs to Jamie in Chelmsford. I'll go with you tomorrow."

Mike has a different idea: "I'll just drive by tonight after I get out of the prison. I'll be done with work by eleven, and I'll drive past by eleven-thirty. No one will notice me in the dark. I'll just go see what we are dealing with and if the truck is there."

I give him the address, knowing I shouldn't, and make him swear he won't knock on the door. We need to know where she is without her catching on, I explain.

"Please don't do something that will make her take off again," I plead.

The day drags on without a word from her. I go to work and try to appear to do my job. I have conversations that I half-listen to. I remind myself that I have three other children. Liam is away at college and not doing well. He is worried about his sister, his best friend. My two older children do not understand why Katie won't stop. I call Melody and leave a message: "Everything is okay, I was just thinking about you and wanted to say hello." She may or may not call back. The stress of this has been too much for her, and she rarely answers the phone but will check in by text.

Next, I call Liam. "Hey, sweetie, how are you?"

"I'm good, Mom, how are you?"

"I'm good," I lie, grateful that he accepts it.

"Tell me what's going on with you," I say, and then listen to the day-to-day, all is so very normal. He talks about school, homework, how his car needs a tire, says that he's been getting to the gym every day. It all sounds like the best day I've ever heard of, and I'm so glad that he has gotten to experience it.

There is no point in checking in with my older son. He has distanced himself from the chaos. I can't change that, so I try to accept it.

Mike texts me at ten-thirty, saying he can't stand it any longer and is leaving work early. He will call me from in front of the house. Eleven-fifteen, the time he should have arrived, comes and goes, then eleven-thirty. I'm scared. The man drives me nuts, but I don't want anything to happen to him. Thoughts cascade through my head. I picture him looking in a window and finding Katie's dead body. I imagine that he runs into drug dealers and they shoot him. Or he approaches the house as a john is entering and Mike kills the man with his bare hands.

Just when I can't stand it any longer, my phone rings. Instead of Mike, it is Katie, hysterical and screaming so that I can't make out what she's saying.

"Slow down, slow down. I can't understand you."

"He busted down the fucking door. He embarrassed me in front of people, and he destroyed the door. If someone calls the police, they are going to arrest me. I have warrants. I hate him. Why is he here? I am not going with him. I'm not leaving Chad, and I'm not going with him. He's fucking crazy and I'm fine. I AM FINE!"

"Okay, calm down, honey, your father and I are just worried about you," I say in my most mollifying voice. "Now maybe if you are concerned about the police coming, you should pull yourself together?"

In the background, I hear Mike's Irish brogue, which thickens when he's mad. I can imagine Mike peering in the window and then, outfitted like he's part of a SWAT team, in black boots and prison officer's garb, kicking the door in. Yes, I'm pretty sure I didn't need to be there to know what happened. I'm only missing the insane details. Mike takes the phone.

"What happened to the plan to find out where she's staying so we can section her tomorrow morning?" I ask.

"I saw her through the window in this fucking crack house, and I couldn't just drive by. When I knocked on the door, they didn't answer fast enough, so I kicked the fucking thing in."

"Michael, what the fuck? How fast was fast enough? What's to keep her from taking off now?"

"She's with Chad and that piece of shit from the last treatment center, Jamie—you were right. Isn't that great, introduced to more junkies? No furniture, just a bunch of them shooting up. She's out of her mind. She won't come with me."

The word *junkies* pierces me. I can still hear her crying and carrying on in the background, amid sounds of confusion and panic. I know Mike well enough to guess that in mid-knock, he was already kicking the door off its hinges. I also can hear the cocaine or meth mixed with heroin in Katie's voice, quick and gravelly. I'm not sure how to calm the situation from forty miles away while the phone is being tossed back and forth like a hot potato.

"What do you mean she won't come with you?" I ask Mike. "What are you going to do? You can't leave her there!"

"The only thing I can do is call the police and turn her in for the warrants. I can't make her get in the car if she won't. Your call; tell me what you want me to do."

"Are you serious? I want you to go back in time to two hours ago and follow the goddamn plan we had, that's what I want you to do. Don't put me in charge after you fucked it up. Let me talk to her."

Speaking in the same monotone voice I've trained myself to use with Katie, I ask her to please relax and remind her that there's a warrant out for her arrest. Then I tell her that we will be back for her the following morning. I pray she has nowhere else to go.

Pulling up to the complex the following morning, I'm struck by how ordinary it all is: a tricycle in the front yard next door, a group of landscapers trimming the lawns across the complex, kids playing hopscotch in a driveway across the street. No one driving by in the light of day would have known what was going on in this house, but I doubt that anyone, after last night's ruckus, is unaware now.

After having spoken to Chad's parents only on the phone, Mike and I have arranged to meet them down the street. They look like any of my well-dressed, upper-middle-class neighbors. We talk briefly, then call each of our kids individually while driving to the house. Katie answers, and she is calmer than she was last night, but surprised that we are here. She comes out, dirty and with her hair pinned up. She's wearing Chad's long-sleeved sweatshirt and sweatpants and carrying a single bag.

"Where are all of your clothes?" I ask.

She looks down at her bare feet and whispers, "Gone."

"Again?" I ask, not expecting an answer. Of course they are gone; the real question is, why do I keep replacing them?

All the fight has left her. She embraces Chad, the guy who up until recently had been driving her to her "dates" so that she could afford to buy them both heroin. They cry and swear to each other that they will be together when they get clean. If not for knowing the situation, you would imagine that perhaps one of them is going off on a long trip, maybe to a faraway college, or being shipped out to Afghanistan. It's only the smell of withdrawal and drugs coming through their pores, the obvious stench from not having bathed in what appears to be more than a week, and their worn, sunken-eyed faces that tell the true story.

We parents have little to say to one another. What is there to say, after all? We both want to blame the other child, and we both know it's our own child that's the problem. Mike has already called the insurance company to ask where to bring Katie, and they have informed him that she is covered for inpatient detox at McLean Hos-

pital in Belmont. He has let them know she will do the intake paperwork on the ride to the hospital. I watch Mike drive away with her
and see him hand her the phone to complete the intake.

The townhouse has been quiet, but now I see a girl, no older than
Katie, peering through a crack in the blinds. *Whose child are you?* I
think. *Who is awake all night remembering your childhood with a broken heart?* She sees me looking at her, and we lock eyes for a second.
Please come out and get in my car. I'll take you home, I think. A child's
ball bounces off my car and I turn my head at the sound; when I look
back, she is gone. My eyes follow the ball and then the child, maybe
five or six years old, blond hair swinging behind her, chasing it. I wonder if she will grow up to be addicted to heroin. I realize at this point
that I may never look at a child in any other way.

Taking a deep breath, I start the car and go to work.

I've heard from Katie once, so I believe that she is still at McLean,
while inwardly fearing that she is not. She hasn't signed a release for
us to speak with anyone, so I'm not sure from moment to moment if
she is safe. McLean will give her a maximum of seven days to detox,
and then she must go somewhere else. The only place I know is the
facility she was at last time that didn't seem to do anything other than
introduce her to new people to use with.

I've been speaking with Matt the Poet and now am also in contact with Mike Duggan from Wicked Sober, two of Marion's suggestions from that first night at Learn to Cope. Katie's dad has also
been speaking with Mike Duggan. Both Matt and Mike Duggan are
suggesting Florida for rehab. My head is spinning, and I only have
days to figure it all out. Katie, on the other hand, is still nasty and
not wanting to stay in detox. She tells me nothing about herself when
she calls, only asks about Chad. I hold in all impulses to scream at

her because I want her to finish her stay at McLean and I'm all too aware that she can leave at any time.

Mike and I agree to meet at McLean for visiting hours the day before she is scheduled to leave. I make my way up the hill and the front steps of a building that looks more like an old asylum from a black-and-white photograph. Everything about the outside, as well as the inside, is old and bare and scary. I can't believe my sweet girl has just spent six days here.

Not seeing Mike's car in the small visitors' parking lot, I conclude that I have arrived first. I approach the receptionist and speak Katie's name through a slot in a Plexiglas window. A young woman in scrubs instructs me to have a seat and points to several hard, molded-plastic orange chairs right out of the seventies. I stand in the corner of the room and wait. It is too familiar and reminds me of the methadone clinic my grandmother attended a lifetime ago.

A burly man in scrubs opens the door, and behind him, I see Katie. I am shocked at how thin and tiny she looks. Her face has broken out, and her long hair is a tangled mess, held back by a large clip. Her arms, exposed in a short-sleeved shirt, are destroyed. Track marks cover both of them, mostly the left. A bandage obscures what I will later find out is an abscess, caused by shooting up. She looks at me and starts to cry.

"Mommy, I hate it here. Please let me go home."

My heart splinters into a thousand pieces. Everything in me wants to scoop her up and travel back in time to before all this happened, to take her home and protect her from herself. Both Matt and Mike Duggan had warned me that this would happen. Though neither explicitly told me not to take her home, both cautioned me that she needed more treatment and told me stories of parents who regretted the decision to forgo further treatment after their child had pleaded to go home.

The mother in me wants nothing more than to have the child I knew and loved back in her own bedroom. But I understand that the reality of the situation is that the child doesn't exist anymore. If I want any version of Katie back ever again, I have to be strong and insist on treatment.

I change the subject to her hair. She had asked me earlier in the week if I could bring a brush and detangling spray, which I did. Now she leads me to her room, little more than a cell, which until that morning she'd shared with another woman, who has just been discharged. I get situated on her bed—it is hard and covered with a plastic bed cover that crinkles under my weight—and she sits in front of me on yet another orange plastic chair. I unclip her hair and wait for it to fall so I can begin.

I am without words. Her hair, once a beautiful chestnut brown that flowed down her back, stays exactly as it had when it was held up by the clip. I try to loosen it, but it is completely matted to her head, like a feral dog's fur. It takes all my strength not to cry.

"It's bad, isn't it?" she asks.

"It's not good" is all I can say.

She begins to cry again and I assure her, lying as best I can, that with all the conditioners I brought she can loosen the knots in the shower and slowly work them out, but she doesn't believe it, and neither do I. She puts the useless clip back in her hair, pretending that even her hair is all right, and we are directed toward the family room, where her father is now waiting.

As we enter the room, I am thankful to see worn, threadbare couches instead of unyielding plastic furniture. Mike is seated, as is a young guy he is speaking with. Katie is clearly suspicious but goes to hug her father.

"Hi, Katie, I'm Mike Duggan. Maureen, it's nice to finally meet you in person."

"Oh, my God, it's so good to meet you," I gush.

After speaking with Mike over the last few weeks, I'd gotten to feel like I knew him, but I hadn't been picturing the clean-cut guy now before me. He looks more like a high school history teacher than someone recovering from a heroin addiction. Katie's father had had a quick conversation with our new friend earlier this morning, on his way to the hospital, and Mike Duggan had offered to drive over and help us talk to Katie.

"I am happy to help," he had told my ex. "Sometimes they will listen to someone who has been through it before they will listen to their parents."

He focuses on Katie now. "I've been speaking with your mom and dad over the last couple of weeks because they've been concerned, as you know. I want you to know that I've been sober for four years and I found my sobriety in Florida. I founded a nonprofit called Wicked Sober when I returned to Boston to help other people get into treatment. What are your plans after leaving here tomorrow?"

Katie is not interested in telling anyone her plans.

"Katie, you know your father's house is not a good option," I chime in, unable to stay quiet. "Marblehead is not a good idea right now, either. Chad's parents are sending him somewhere, and they said he'd be gone as long as possible."

Chad's parents and Mike and I had talked among ourselves about how to keep Katie and Chad separated, so I tell Katie that I have no idea where he is going. "We can talk about you coming home if you get further treatment and can stay sober for a period of time," I add.

"I am not going back to that last treatment center. It didn't help. I know *you* wanted it to, but it didn't."

Mike Duggan talks to Katie, explaining what he has gone through, how bad it had gotten. He had suffered a sports injury and gotten hooked on painkillers, then moved on to heroin in college, quickly failing out. He had alienated everyone he cared about, watched his friends die, stolen from everyone he could, ruined everything in his path, and nearly lost his own life. He would never have imagined that he would now be a married man with a child, helping other people.

"It's possible, Katie," he says. "People do get well and get it all back. I know it doesn't feel possible now, but look at me if you need proof."

I'm not sure whether it is what he says or the way he says it, but Katie suddenly deflates, and then she acquiesces. It is as though he has spoken some magical words, some secret language that only heroin addicts can understand, that convinces her to give in and go.

Not wasting any time, we book a flight to Florida and make the arrangements while standing in the cramped counselor's office. McLean is a trusted name, and we take the clinicians' recommendation, hoping Katie will be getting the best treatment possible. She'll be leaving for Fort Lauderdale the next day. I kiss her good-bye and say, "I love you."

I once again try to comfort myself with the thought that it can't possibly get any worse than this, even though each time I've done that, it somehow has. Homeless and dirty, with matted hair—this must be her rock bottom. She's lost everything except us. All the dreams have changed, mine and hers. I am grieving for someone who is still alive.

five | Fall

B rian, Marion's son, is doing better. He is in a halfway house in Boston, and Marion speaks of him the way some people might talk about their child at Yale. They still watch any sport with a ball together: Celtics, Red Sox, Pats. He is on the upswing, and she feels comfortable enough to plan to leave for a few days in early October to attend the Fed Up! rally in Washington, D.C., which will become most known for the surgeon general's acknowledgment that addiction is a disease. Her happiness gives me happiness; her hope is contagious.

"Katie has been gone for nearly a month," I explain to Marion when she asks why I'm not joining her on the bus I've helped charter through Magnolia. "I'm planning on visiting her for her birthday on the fifteenth; I'll be just coming back from Florida when the rally starts. I can't believe my trip is just a little over a week away!"

"Understandable. Are you nervous to see her? How does she sound?" Marion is laconic and rarely uses a misplaced word.

We have all become insanely attuned to the sounds of our children.

Wrong as often as we are right, we listen for changes in their voices, hints of relapse or mentioning of people who may be a bad influence. We are always trying to catch them before they fall, much as we did when they were little and swinging from monkey bars.

"She sounds happy," I tell Marion. "She's completed the inpatient program and moved on to the outpatient one at Banyan. She complained at first that the housing wasn't in such a great neighborhood, but she seems to be starting to like it now that she's making friends. I miss her even more now that she's starting to sound like herself again."

I'm antsy, and I walk through my house and into the room that was once Katie's. Maybe I am nervous, just like Marion suggested. The walls, once decorated with a border of dancing bears, since outgrown, were long ago painted blue. Her girly white furniture has been removed, and when she moved in with Chad, she took or threw out almost everything else, leaving only some of the more sentimental childhood memories behind at my request. Garshew the Cat, who has seen better days, sits on a high shelf, a lonely reminder of the little girl who would have entire conversations with him. The room is otherwise empty of her now, except for some long-ignored softball trophies, framed family photos, and a painting she bought when we went to the Dominican Republic for her twenty-first birthday.

I had always tried to make birthdays memorable, overcompensating for the lack of attention mine received when I was growing up, and we had planned that one together. My favorite birthday with Katie was probably her eighteenth. She loved Florida and had spent a lot of time there after my father passed away, leaving a condo in Naples that we eventually had to sell. She knew she was going somewhere, but not until I woke her up at five a.m.—singing "Happy Birthday," as I did for all four of my children each birthday morning—did I reveal that we were going to stay right on the beach in Naples, on the west coast of Florida.

She jumped out of bed with utter delight. We stopped to get an iced coffee, which she drank no matter the season, and she announced to the entire store that she was off to Florida for her birthday. The workers clapped and sang "Happy Birthday" to her. We had a beautiful "hurricane season special" room where we could step out onto the beach from our sliding glass doors. There were massages and pedicures, and we ate dinner watching the sun set. It was a quick couple of days, but I hold on to memories like that to remind me of the real Katie. The Katie I imagined finishing college, landing her first serious job, then getting married in a storybook wedding and having babies I'd eventually spoil with too much chocolate and who would love to stay the night at their grandma's house in the room that was once hers.

The empty room is source of pain each time I pass by it. I close my eyes and stand in the place where I had wished her a thousand sweet dreams. Even the good memories sting. The house is small, and having a room that isn't used doesn't make sense. I had moved the bed down to the condo on the Cape when I realized Katie wouldn't be using it anytime soon, with promises to buy her a new bed when she got back on her feet. I had realized that the sensible thing to do would be to close the office I've been working from in Salem and move everything into this room, but I haven't yet done that. I'll need to start paying for Katie's sober living arrangements as the end of the insured portion of her stay quickly approaches.

I close the door as I step out of the room so that I won't have to look at what I am leaving behind.

———

'm on the phone with a sales rep from my cable company, who is trying to explain that it is somehow cheaper if I add more services to my plan, when the phone beeps, signaling another call—a Florida number. I quickly disconnect the sales rep, losing my shot at HBO, to find Katie crying on the other end of the line. Not the routine crying I am becoming numb to but the "something awful has happened" crying I have learned to decipher. They are making her leave Banyan, she tells me, just a week before her birthday.

"Leave? What do you mean, leave? We are paying for this. We are paying A LOT for this. How can they make you leave?"

Actually, it is still our insurance that is paying for it but it's her dad's plan, so I am indignant on behalf of Harvard Pilgrim.

I have been trying to get Katie's counselor on the phone for days. She had called once to check in with me when Katie first arrived, sounding all peppy and promising to let me know how she was doing, now that a release had been signed. I haven't heard a word from her since then, and my calls have gone unanswered. I sit down hard on the couch, put the phone on speaker, and hold my pounding head in my hands.

"They think I'm hanging around with people who have relapsed. It's not true, either. I was in Tommy's car and we stopped to say hello to two of Justin's friends in front of the house they rent. How was I supposed to know they had been at Banyan and relapsed?"

"Who the fuck are Justin and Tommy and why are you riding around in a car with them? You're supposed to be in treatment!"

The phone immediately goes dead. I call her back. Voice mail. I text her. No answer. I call the peppy counselor. Nothing. I call the main office and ask to speak to the CEO. He is in a meeting with the peppy counselor. I call Matt and ask him to get an answer for me.

Matt is the only person who returns my call, later that day. Katie has already been transferred to A Rainbow Start, a treatment program where Banyan sometimes sends clients. There's nothing he can do about it. He explains that this was the second time she was seen near a known drug house, so the Banyan staffers feel that for her own good, she should be out of that area.

"Why didn't they give me the opportunity to decide where she should go?" I ask. "I don't appreciate how she was traded off to the minors without so much as a phone call."

"I don't know. I'm not happy about this, either."

"So, what do I do? What do I do next?" I had been planning on visiting Katie the following week, but Matt tells me there is often a blackout period during which patients are not allowed visitors; he advises me to call and check into it. He gives me the number, and I leave a message with all my contact information.

Finally, after several calls to the clinical director, I get a call back from A Rainbow Start on September 11, four days before Katie's birthday.

"She's doing great and is making terrific progress, cooperative and engaged. We are happy to have her here. She has a special fondness for art therapy. She's very talented," she explains.

I have always thought this is true, and I'm thrilled that Katie is finding something she enjoys again. I recall all the art classes I paid for and think how they are finally paying for themselves. Maybe this is for the best.

"Kaitlin is picked up every day for outpatient programming," the director tells me, "and given rides to meetings in the evening."

It is the facility's clinical director who is meeting with Katie in the absence of her assigned counselor, who met with her once on the first day and will be back next week. The director reassures me that

Katie is doing well and says there shouldn't be any problem with my taking her away from the facility for a couple of nights for her birthday. I am flooded with relief and feel myself tear up.

"She hasn't been calling me, just a couple of texts," I explain, "so I was worried."

"Nothing to worry about, I assure you. Kaitlin is fine."

I hang up the phone and text my girl: "I love you. Just talked to Rainbow Start and they said you are doing great."

The counselors there may not be the best at getting back to me, but they certainly know my daughter. I'm so pleased that she sounds like herself again. So what if I need to be a pest to get an answer when the answers are as good as that?

"I love you too," she replies.

I'm looking forward to our vacation. I hope it will be like the Dominican Republic two years before, when she turned twenty-one. A few days of lying on the beach, reminding her what life can be like, and then hopefully she will finish up in Florida and come home, herself again. Finally seeing a light at the end of the tunnel, I begin to relax and get back to my own life. I picture her healthy and happy.

Having joined enough Facebook groups to keep me plugged in twenty-four hours a day, I start to investigate Florida and find people who live down there and others who have sent their children to treatment. There are good and bad stories. I only really focus on the bad ones. It is impossible to know who to trust.

In the Facebook groups that are staffed with volunteer administrators who pay attention, I find a lot of support but a serious lack of information. Caution over promoting any one treatment center had turned into controlled overprotection that prevented anyone from openly sharing information. But I need answers, not prayers.

There are followers, like groupies, of certain self-proclaimed advocates. With little or no education—or, in some cases, not even personal experience with addiction themselves—these leaders report on missing person searches, interventions, and saving of lives. One local tattooed savior became involved in a nonprofit and began independently collecting donations. I cynically suspect that the donations are going toward more tattoos.

The treatment industry seems to attract egomaniacs. Some former addicts and mothers of addicts become obsessed with the notoriety that comes with helping people get into treatment and then, all too often, are corrupted by the large sums of money paid to the worst of them from various treatment centers hoping to cater to those who trust these helpers—all a harbinger of future abuses. Relapsing kids are bounced back and forth between facilities, earning someone a commission each time and a hefty insurance payout to the facility. There are rumors of kids far from home paid to relapse, or housed in shady facilities that bill their insurances for urine and drug screens that are never conducted. I hear about sober houses that are far from sober.

Many people claim to be saving lives, and they are all on Facebook telling how they did it—the more dramatic the story, the better. It feels wrong. People at the most desperate times in their lives are being targeted by these carpetbaggers. These vultures with no conscience are trying to make a quick buck, and the parents of addicts are easy prey, desperate and grasping at anyone who claims to know more than they do.

I need someone to tell me if I am doing the right or wrong things, if Katie is in good hands and what to do next. Instead, I read an endless stream of heartbreaking tales of relapse and loss and prayers being sent from others who have been down the same road. I find the most vocal members of the groups and contact them via Messenger, asking to talk to them and looking for answers. I find people in Massachusetts and Florida willing to share their experiences. I am developing connections, and many of these people are looking for the same kind of help I am—better information, and contact with other people going through the same crises.

Watching what others are going through makes me want to change the mission of Magnolia slightly. There are so many people who have no information available to them and lack the money to help their children—not to mention the children who have worn their families out and are no longer welcome in their lives. All of these people need a safe place to ask for information from their peers, a place that is free of anyone trying to make money off them. Somewhere trusted.

I learn of programs in Massachusetts where I could have sent Katie. Places where she wouldn't have been so far away. There are kids stranded all around the country, sent by well-meaning parents, often with the assistance of not so well-meaning "saviors," and then unable to afford to come home. And there are also people who have completed programs but have nowhere to go after treatment.

It is Monday morning, September 14, 2015: the day before I leave for Florida, and the day before Katie's birthday. I'm busily packing, distracted with all that needs to be done before I leave; I barely notice that she has texted me only a few times over the weekend. She sounded good though, excited to see me and looking forward to her birthday. Tuesday morning can't come fast enough.

The house phone rings, and I look at the caller ID to see if it's one of my kids or a telemarketer. Though I don't recognize the number, I answer in case it has something to do with Katie.

"Hello, can I speak with Maureen?"

"Oh, boy. This is Maureen."

"Maureen, this is Marisol from It's Your Time sober living in Lake Worth."

I had been told that Katie was at A Rainbow Start's sober living facility, so my defenses are immediately raised.

"I want to let you know that Katie left the house on Thursday evening and did not return. We have her belongings packed, and we would like to know when someone will be available to pick them up?"

"That's not possible," I say. "I just spoke to A Rainbow Start's clinical director on Friday, and she told me that Katie was there that day, doing an art project, and that she could come with me for a couple of days. I spoke with her several times last week."

"Katie Harvey?" she asks.

"Yes, Kaitlin Harvey from Massachusetts."

"The Katie Harvey who was here was scheduled for A Rainbow Start, but as far as I can see, she did not attend. She broke curfew the second night she was here and then went out and didn't return on Thursday. The treatment center should have been in touch with you."

I take down Marisol's number and tell her I'll call her right back. I frantically dial the clinical director, who picks up on the second ring. Thank God, I can straighten this out quickly. I stop packing and walk outside to sit on my front steps. In the rest of the world, people are going about their day, ferrying kids to school, heading to the gym or to work, or walking the dog. I long for boredom.

"Hello, this is Maureen Cavanagh, Katie Harvey's mom," I say. "I just got a call from a Marisol at It's Your Time, and she is stating that Katie has been missing since Thursday. I've explained to her that you and I have been talking all last week and that Katie is doing well, but she insists that Katie's belongings need to be moved out and that she hasn't attended A Rainbow Start."

"Did you say Katie Harvey?" the director slowly asks.

"Yes, Kaitlin Harvey. Katie, who has been doing art projects and who I am coming to see tomorrow and taking to Singer Island for two days for her birthday."

"Can you please hold on, Ms. Cavanagh?" the director asks, then puts me on hold before I can respond.

Can I hold on? I wonder, *Exactly how long can I hold on?*

"What the fuck, what the fuck, what the fuck," I whisper under my breath. I know something is wrong, but I can't even imagine what it is. I have been a good, if not squeaky, parent. I asked everyone I could about the center, I called every other day, and I stayed in touch with Katie. What did I miss?

The director gets back on the phone and asks if she can put me on speaker. My stomach does a flip, and I open the screen door and head inside to sit down on the couch. "Your daughter came in last week for the initial intake," the director tells me, "but it appears as though she was accidentally left off the pickup list for our transportation and never came back after the first day."

"You have got to be kidding!" I scream. "I trusted you with my child, and you told me long stories about how she was doing and how she was looking forward to me visiting. You said she was doing well!"

"Apparently, there was a mix-up," she admits, "and I was updating you on another Kaitlin who came in on the same day."

"Are you fucking kidding me?" I ask. "Do you realize that anything could be happening to her right now? She's been gone since Thursday, you fucking idiot. I want to speak with your boss. I want answers as to how this could happen. I am going to see that this place is closed down unless someone calls me right the fuck now and tells me they are going to find my daughter!"

"I will have someone call you right a—"

I hear only part of her answer as I hang up the phone and call Katie. Her phone goes right to voice mail, which means it's either off or dead. I pray that only the phone is dead.

I call Marisol back and tell her what happened. She is the house manager at It's Your Time and sounds only slightly older than Katie. She doesn't seem surprised.

"I've packed her things up, and I'll leave them in the garage for you. I did find heroin and needles in her room, just so you know. I will call you if I hear anything," she promises.

I t is September 15. Today is Katie's birthday, and I'm up and out at the same time we headed to Logan airport for her birthday just a year before. Katie texted me last night that she was doing well and had a good day in her program. She obviously has no idea that I know she has left, and I decide to keep it that way.

I manage to get Wi-Fi on the plane and watch for responses to a Facebook post with Katie's picture and a Missing headline in an online parent support group. Her description and last known where-abouts have been shared via The Addict's Mom group across Florida and are being passed through the entire mom network. No one has seen her, but I'm offered words of encouragement, horror stories, and more prayers. Dazed, I feel less alone, though no less frightened.

Finally, the plane lands, and I text Katie to ask her how she is. Standing on line in the plane's center aisle with happy vacationing families and retirees returning to their snowbird homes away from home, I force myself not to come apart. An obviously overtired two-year-old boy who has cried through most of the flight lies down on the floor in front of me, kicking his feet and screaming, "I don't want to." There is nothing I'd like to do more than join him. I completely understand how he feels and give him the thumbs-up.

Having secured my rental car, I begin to drive to the address Marisol has provided for the sober house. I've been texting Katie without any reply, but it's still only ten a.m., so she may be asleep, I tell myself. Asleep where, I don't allow myself to think about for too long. About fifteen minutes away from the house, the phone rings, and it is Katie.

"Hi, Mommy."

"Hey, baby, what are you up to?" I manage to maintain my composure and neither scream at her to tell me where she is nor burst into tears because I'm finally speaking to her.

"Not much, just chillin'," she responds.

I keep her on the line and make small talk, meanwhile shushing the GPS, which tells me I have only two miles to go before my destination.

"I can't wait to see you tomorrow," she says.

"I'm here now, honey. I just got here—remember, I was coming on your birthday so we would be together and I could sing 'Happy Birthday'?"

"You're here? Now? Wait, today is my birthday? I thought it was tomorrow."

A small bit of panic followed by clarity infiltrates her voice.

"Where are you, sweetie? I know you haven't been at the house. Tell me where you are so that I can come get you."

"I'm fine, Mom, really, it's a long story but I'm really fine. I was with my friend Kevin. I didn't like the house, but I'm good. I promise, don't worry. I'm just going to the house to get my clothes now."

"I know," I say. "Turn around, I'm in the driveway."

Katie is just climbing the front steps to the ramshackle, Caribbean-pink ranch that looks like every other house nearby. None of them strike me as a place you'd want to leave your child. A palm tree is positioned in the front yard in the same spot at each house on the block.

At It's Your Time, Christmas lights wrap around the porch railing—a remnant left behind by a much happier resident. A white sheet covers the front window where blinds or curtains belong, and one plastic pink flamingo leans over, nearly to the ground, as if he is pecking at feed. The house manager meets Katie at the doorway; she is weary and frail, no more than twenty-five, and glances over Katie's shoulder as I pull in the driveway.

The groups of people hanging around the park across the street are reminiscent of the addicts at the park in Salem where Katie used to buy drugs. We've come twelve hundred miles for a different version of the same thing. Katie spots me getting out of the unfamiliar car, phone still to her ear, and runs toward me. She's wearing a sundress I've never seen. The memory of a three-year-old Katie in the flowered dress she insisted on calling a "fun dress" rather than a sundress pops into my head. I throw the phone down on the seat of the LeBaron convertible I had arranged to rent weeks ago, because Katie always wanted to ride in a convertible, and hug her as hard as I can without hurting her.

We pile bags of clothes into the trunk of the car and head toward the beach. I refuse to ask any questions; they will just be met with lies. My mind is racing, putting together a plan. She talks about what she wants to eat for dinner and falls asleep as we drive.

If it weren't for the fact that Katie is nodding in and out of consciousness, it would be a lovely drive to Singer Island. I don't bother putting the car's top down; she hasn't even noticed that we're in a convertible. When I pull up to the valet, I shake her awake.

"Will you be staying with us, ma'am?" asks a cute kid, full of muscles and smelling of aftershave, about twenty-two years old, and he looks over at Katie. She's still beautiful, even though her hair needed to be cut short, almost to the scalp, after she left McLean; bottles of conditioner and a trip to the hairdresser couldn't budge the knots and matted clumps. Katie turned that misfortune into an adorable pixie cut.

Katie comes to, confused and not quite sure where she is, and gives the valet a once-over that makes me uncomfortable. Everything she does feels like an opportunity to get drugs, so I rush her to the front desk, insist on carrying our bags, and press the button to close the elevator door.

On the eleventh floor, the view from the room is magnificent, nothing but ocean and sky. Katie has immediately curled up with her phone, totally uninterested in the room, the windows, or the view. Once again, taking advantage of hurricane season, I have sprung for a suite with a view. Off to the left, the pools are visible, all three of them. The bathroom is marble and bigger than Katie's childhood bedroom. Just a few short years ago, Katie would have been out of her mind with excitement, begging to go the pool, asking for a pedicure, or running to the beach. The windows span the entire two rooms, and the sun is dropping slightly in the sky, signaling that this shitty day may finally be coming to a close. It's four thirty, and I want to sleep and wake up tomorrow with none of this ever having happened.

"I'm starving. I haven't eaten in, like, three days."

I tell her to go take a shower first, because if she hasn't eaten in three days, my guess is that she hasn't showered in many more than that. This will also give me a chance to search the bags she brought with her.

She obliges, and when I hear the shower running, I pull apart the small duffel bag I've never seen before. It's filled with clothes that smell like body odor, the whites and the colors all dull and gray from lack of washing. Nothing looks familiar. At the very bottom, there is a glass frame with WELCOME TO DISNEY WORLD written across the top.

She's been carrying around a photo of her and Liam with Mickey Mouse ears from a trip the three of us took to Orlando when she was eight and Liam was five. I hold the photo close to my heart and remember waking them up—another surprise, bags packed while they were at school—to tell them we were going to Disney World. We stayed on the resort property, taking the early tram to a different part of the park each morning and then coming back to swim until dark. They ate hamburgers and drank grape soda for breakfast, lunch, and dinner, and the only TV anyone watched was the Disney Channel. What I wouldn't do to go back to that vacation.

The water stops, and I put everything back and make a quick search through her purse, finding nothing that looks like drugs.

Wrapped in a plush white towel, her head turbaned in another, she pops out of the bathroom looking more upbeat.

"Salmon! I've been thinking about eating salmon. Do you think they will have it in the restaurant downstairs?"

We have to walk around the property several times before the restaurant opens, at five. Katie is noticeably messed up, so much so that she leaves her arms uncovered, letting me see fresh track marks. She gazes at the pool and the beach and talks about a tomorrow that I know will not happen. I listen and promise nothing. Finally, it is time for dinner, and she eats like a person who indeed has not seen food for three days. Hardly talking, because there is nothing safe to say, I listen to her tell me about her friend Kevin, but she strategically omits any mention of drugs.

I scan the other people in the restaurant, who do not have a heroin-addicted child sitting next to them, who don't worry if every day might be their child's last, who will not be hunting for another treatment center the following day. I catch the eye of a woman a few tables away who is watching Katie enjoy her dinner, surely not knowing what is really going on. She smiles at me, and I muster a smile back.

Katie falls asleep almost immediately after dinner, and this year I sing "Happy Birthday" to her while she sleeps. I spend most of the night texting people for advice and watching to make sure Katie hasn't snuck out in the middle of the night or stopped breathing next to me. The morning comes too quickly, and her mood changes to sullen and difficult. Finally, there is no avoiding talking to her about what is next.

"We need to either bring you back to Massachusetts and find a place for you or take a look at some other places in Florida," I say. "I can't leave you down here without a place to live."

Katie can't disagree with that. She agrees to look but doesn't agree to check in anywhere.

"We're just looking, right?"

"Yes, just looking."

After breakfast, we have the car brought around, and she gapes at it as if she's never seen it before.

"A convertible? You got a convertible?"

"You're only twenty-three once," I say. The last word catches in my throat. I allow myself to wonder for a second if she will ever see twenty-four.

For a moment, the excitement of the car takes over, and we pull the top down and hit the road. Her short hair blows in the wind, and she looks like a version of herself again. She raises her arms, covered in a light long-sleeved shirt, and the tattoo she got sometime while she was missing in Massachusetts, "freedom" written across her wrist, is visible behind the gauzy material. Just an inch or so higher, past the tiny birds flying above that single word, are the track marks that contradict the optimism of the tattoo, which she got to remind

herself that she wants to break free from heroin. I turn back to the
road and step on the gas, and we cruise over the causeway, with her
laughter ringing in my ears.

That afternoon, the laughter stops. What I had presented as "just
looking," a college tour, has ended abruptly at the first treatment
center, known for its music therapy approach. I imagined that the
recording studio, instruments, and famous names associated with
the center might be enough to convince her to stay. I can see she is
beginning to get sick, and if I knew any better, I would recognize
the symptoms of withdrawal. The ordinariness of the building belies
the activity within.

Gold records adorn the walls of Recovery Unplugged, along with
autographed guitars played by members of Aerosmith and other bands
I recall mostly from my own youth.

Isaac, a good-natured and seasoned veteran of the treatment industry, offers to show Katie around, and in doing so, he manages to get
her to admit that she has needles and heroin in the trunk of the car.

"You promised that you wouldn't leave me here," she snaps at me.
"I would have never come if I knew I had to stay."

I am starting to get upset when Isaac encourages me to say good-
bye. She will be fine, he assures me, and another member of the team
will take me to see the house where she will be living later. Katie defi-
antly pulls her belongings out of the trunk and hands them over to
Isaac. She asks for a cigarette, puts it between her lips, and lights it,
something I have never seen her do before. It hangs from her lip like
she's been smoking for forty years, and she reminds me of someone I
used to know long ago: my mother. That makes it just a little easier to
say good-bye.

Katie hugs me quickly and walks back into Recovery Unplugged without turning around. I stand in the parking lot and stare at the building, which looks like any other office building but holds the hopes and dreams of some forty-five parents. The palm trees sway in the breeze, a perfect beach day. Twenty-three years before, Mike and I had taken home our sweet baby girl, only a day old, her brother and sister eager to welcome her. Where had we gone wrong?

I can see the water from the parking lot. Katie will have a view of the bay and in any other circumstance, that would be exciting. So much has happened in such a short period of time, and it is all finally hitting me. I pull the roof of the car back up, not in the mood for the breeze or the beach, and go back to the hotel and climb into bed. I will sleep on the side of the bed that held my daughter until it is time to leave for the airport the following day. That night, I sob for the first time in a long time: for the loss of the child I knew, for all my hopes and dreams that may never happen, for my own life, which will never be the same. It's all too much. I weep for her as well, and I know that, miles away, she is crying, too.

six

Winter 2016

Katie's old bedroom sits empty, taunting me to come in. I walk by it instead. Still, I see the hardwood floor gleaming, the closet completely empty of the masses of clothes she'd pile inside it when I'd finally demand that she clean her room, her trophies and Garshew still sitting high on the shelf that rings the room. The door is closed, but I know it's all still there.

Over the last year, I've ignored my insurance business, and my income has taken a hit. With Katie in Florida, I am slowly beginning to get things back on track. My office space, with its industrial feel and exposed brick walls, has to go. The upside: I won't have to drive, twice a day, past the apartment building where Katie was arrested. The plan is to split the office furniture between my house and Randy's house and to move my business into what is now the spare room. Katie's room.

I console myself with jokes about the easier commute and working in my pajamas, but it's disappointing. I'm also worried about being alone so much, even though Liam is now back home, having left the

University of New Hampshire to attend school locally. With the difference in tuition and Katie safe, I'm hoping that the added savings of working at home will allow me to pull my business out of the toilet and work on the nonprofit.

As the office move date approaches, I'm paralyzed. Randy takes charge and pushes me to pick a color so he can start painting. I can't help him because of the guilt I feel over covering up Katie's paint. I know she can't live with me after she leaves Florida, assuming that she returns, but with each brushstroke, I feel the young, sweet girl I know slipping away.

The large bedroom window—which, I recently learned, Katie had snuck out of at night—looks over a rock garden that will soon smell of lavender and lilacs. Nearby, a rhododendron given to me years ago by my older daughter, Melody, for Mother's Day blooms a brilliant pink in the spring. Dear God, what will spring bring this year?

I watch Randy paint, admiring the muscles of his broad shoulders and his six-foot-three frame. I have adored this man since March 2010, nearly six years, and I still feel butterflies when I see him across a room. He is the logical, serious, and steady person in the relationship. Whereas I fly by the seat of my pants, he is a calming influence and a realist, offering a counterpart to my idealism, which often borders on the delusional. He is the man your mother wishes you'd marry. The trains run on time in his life because he makes sure they do. He has managed to compromise a lot to accept the chaos of this disease. This fact does not escape me.

I'm well aware of what happens to even the best of relationships in the wake of addiction. Marriages disintegrate, friendships are broken, and family members drift away. One of the great blessings of my life has been this man who stands by me, and by Katie.

He was the first person I shared my concerns about Katie with, and he sprang into action, immediately researching groups, resources, and medical advice. He listens to every detail of each new catastrophe and disappointment, and he holds his tongue as I become freshly hopeful each time there's the slightest sign of a positive shift, and then again when it falls apart.

For all of these reasons, I watch him.

"What do you think?" Randy asks.

"It looks great. I'm going to love working in here."

The rock wall is still bare in spots, with small patches of snow. I have positioned my desk directly in front of the window, where Katie's bed sat a year before, with the view of the rock garden. I try to work, unsuccessfully. I wait until everything is an emergency before completing anything, which is the complete opposite of how I've handled any responsibilities in my life up until now.

I welcome a distraction from work and answer the phone on the first ring when Mike calls. Katie had been doing so well in Florida, but a day before her father and brother visited, for his birthday at the end of November, she slipped up. I thanked God that it wasn't a full-blown relapse and disappearing act. She had been in the next level of treatment and was given a longer leash, and it didn't go well. Luckily, by now I knew exactly what to do, so I made some calls, reached out to a few people I had met in the new Magnolia Facebook group, and had her transferred to a facility that I had heard works with those who have experienced trauma. The prostitution, arrests, and deaths of many friends caused me to believe that Katie qualified. Maybe, I figured, this would do it.

Katie is now enjoying the sun, while we freeze once again in the snow. She bonded at the new place, Ambrosia Treatment Center, with Trish Byars, the counselor assigned to her. Trish is widely known as a no-nonsense, no-bullshit, life changer who will not only call the patient out on their bullshit, but will also be a straight shooter with their parents. After being shut down on the phone for interfering, I look forward to meeting her. She's brilliant.

Mike is calling me now, flustered, after being reprimanded by Trish.

"She's condescending," he complains. "Who does she think she is? I told her she was treating me like a nine-year-old schoolgirl, and do you know what she said?"

"No, but I'm dying to hear."

"She said to stop acting like a nine-year-old schoolgirl then! Who the fuck does she think she is?"

I love Trish. I know she is going to be the change we all need. I feel, for the first time, that Katie is in kind and competent hands. Katie even adores her. Trish is enough like me yet not me, a perfect combination for Katie. At Ambrosia, the counselors have introduced EMDR, a therapeutic method to deal with trauma, and she has started to make real progress.

I have two screens open, and while I work on one, I monitor Facebook on the other. The online Magnolia support groups started on Facebook with just one group and fewer than one hundred people. There were so many online forums, some well-intentioned and helpful, but they didn't give me what I needed, so I assumed they weren't giving others what they needed, either. At crucial times I needed specific information and couldn't find it. I didn't need anyone to do anything for me; I needed to be shown how to help myself, and I wanted that information from people who had been there, like Rhonda and Marion—not from a book or a treatment center but from a peer.

The people on these forums—mostly moms, many of whom had

traveled to Washington, D.C., in October for the rally—were invigorated. They had heard Surgeon General Vivek Murthy speak, and, for the first time for many, had been told that their loved one had a disease. The conversation around the use of stigmatizing language and its effect on how the people we loved were treated by the medical community and society came to the forefront. No more *junkie, addict,* or other demeaning terms. No more hiding in shame because our children, siblings, or parents used drugs. Murthy had explained that although they might have made the unfortunate choice to experiment, their disease had affected and impaired their ability to stop.

He hadn't been offering an excuse or taking away the hope that a person with a substance use disorder—that was the term he chose to use—could be healthy again and maintain their sobriety; instead, he was urging people to understand the brain chemistry that allowed for the disease to manifest initially, and to grasp how incredibly difficult it would be for that person to stop using once they started.

I now see how what I was saying was as important as how I was saying it. Everywhere I look there is an addiction awareness event, a movie showing, a public meeting. Were they there before and I just didn't know how to find them, or is this a new phenomenon? The answer turns out to be a little of both. I set up a table and give out information on Magnolia. *Leap and the net will appear,* I tell myself. I watch the Jim Wahlberg movie *If Only* at showings so many times that I become friendly with him and his assistant Ashley, jokingly asking Jim if I can be cast as the lead if they ever make it into a play.

Little by little, we raise money for Magnolia. My new friends Rhonda and Marion are great supporters, and they are happy to join Magnolia's board of directors. There is so much to do, and most of it requires money. We sell T-shirts, but for the most part we have to approach members of the now-growing Facebook group for donations. Some of the members wish to help other members with the donated funds, which could be a recipe for disaster. We buy a bike for a young man who was in sober living in Florida, and he uses it every day to go to work. We fly several people to Florida for treatment and fly some of them home. We seem to be raising all the money in Massachusetts and spending it in Florida.

I know we need focus, and I also know I need some solid help. Someone who cares about Magnolia's mission as much as I do. That's when I meet Chance Ashman-Galliker in our Facebook group. She has a son who fluctuates between recovery and active addiction, much like Katie, but for the moment he is also doing well.

Always at my desk if not in my car, I speak for hours with Chance on the phone about how the Facebook groups have been both a blessing and a curse. She lives in Maryland and is fairly isolated and envies the in-person relationships I have in Massachusetts. We bond immediately, more like sisters than friends. It is starting to feel like everyone I speak to has a child who is being consumed by heroin. Chance wants to help, and she takes on the role of administrator of the main Facebook support group, accepting members into the group and making sure they follow our guidelines, and ensuring that we deny membership to or quickly eliminate anyone who works for a treatment center and might be trying to sell their services to our members.

As my contacts increase, I find that I know what to do and who to ask for help in Massachusetts, the place where I had been so lost just a short time ago. Facebook is becoming more and more polluted with online advocates and charlatans. We try to stay true to our mission of providing peer support and education. Chance, Rhonda, Marion, and I have a vision of helping to connect people with reliable assistance. We enlist the support of twenty-plus admins, who help run the groups. There are good people doing amazing work, like Chad

Sabora in Missouri, Greg Williams and Jim Hood from Facing Addiction, William White from Illinois, Dr. John Kelly from the Recovery Research Institute, Dr. Ruth Potee in Massachusetts, and so many others.

"If you take the credit for saving someone, then be prepared to take the blame if they don't make it," I angrily explain to one person who claims she is saving lives. "You are merely a traffic cop pointing people in the right direction when you share what you already know. They do all the hard work of saving their own lives." This is important for me to say to others and for me to hear myself.

I get the street version of a master's degree in addiction treatment, with Matt Ganem the Poet as my university. He shows me how to speak to people who are in the throes of the disease and how to help parents differentiate between helping and enabling. I listen to every word like it is gospel and not only share the wisdom but start to implement it in my own life.

My phone rings morning, noon, and night, but my first call is always to Chance. We discuss the latest on the Facebook groups. She works on the groups as if it's her full-time job.

Our biggest concern is financial. When I started Magnolia New Beginnings, I envisioned a small, local nonprofit that would help people who were struggling to start over. The popularity of the Facebook groups is now turning Magnolia into a national organization. People from all over the country have begun to ask for money for transportation to the abundance of treatment centers in Florida in competition with one another; the new centers are offering scholarships to people in return for public thanks from online groups. There is no way to fairly assess if someone is in need. And after the horror show of Katie's disappearance, I have no desire to send anyone out of state, even though at this point she is still doing well at Ambrosia in Florida.

I start to meet with serious advocates and treatment professionals from all over the state and make connections. Seeing what is available in Massachusetts, I feel truly blessed. It is far from perfect, but if you need a detox bed, you can get one in a relatively short amount of time. Yet when I needed it urgently, the information on how to go about doing that was so necessary but so hard to find. Magnolia begins to post a list of open beds every morning.

There is still, however, another huge gap. It is difficult for most people to prolong the time they are in a supported environment after treatment. People are going through programs available through the state, sometimes for up to ninety days, and then returning home or to the street and too often relapsing and starting the cycle all over again—or, worse, dying.

My goal is to bridge that gap. It isn't enough to spend a few days in detox, and it isn't even enough to spend another few weeks in a program. The events that lead to anyone being in a situation where they require treatment for a substance use disorder usually build for a long time. In order to get back to a normal life, that person will need to slowly get back to life as they knew it before—differently. I am beginning to see that it's as much about what happens in treatment as it is about what happens afterward.

Nicole White, who works in treatment and owns sober living houses, once told me she believed that every person in recovery should live in a structured, safe, and supported environment for the first year of recovery, going through every experience a person encounters over that period of time while surrounded by supportive peers. I am seeing this more and more as a huge gap in how we are addressing treatment.

Now, sitting in my office, I hear the postman drop some envelopes into the box. Sorting the household mail from the business mail in my office, I go through the day's assortment of family photo Christmas cards, overdue bills, and holiday merchandising. There's a letter from Katie. I rip it open and eagerly read her familiar handwriting.

Hi Mom,

Today is Sunday, and I have been here a month on Wednesday. That is also 30 days clean. I miss you a lot and feel so fortunate to have such an amazing Mom like you. You are so strong and I am so proud of you for everything that you do. I'm sorry for all of the holidays I have missed in the past year. I wish things weren't this way and I wish I wasn't so sick. I feel helpless. I don't want to do drugs, I don't want to be in jail or institutions, but I don't want to go to "normal" life either. I know you understand the most you possibly can. I've been struggling a lot lately so I'm glad I have an extension. It's hard because I know I'm the only person who can change myself everywhere. I think a lot of the underlying issues are being addressed because emotions are coming out. I just want to do good things with you and I know we will. Thank you for all that you do. You are an amazing and beautiful woman. Things haven't been easy for you and that is what makes you so strong. I hope I can have kids one day and be as good to them as you are to me. Thank you for your unconditional love. Calling you and talking to you on the phone is the best part of my whole week! I hope you are doing things for yourself and not just taking care of everybody else. I can't wait to get the package you sent me. I hope it comes tomorrow.

I've been eating really healthy and trying to exercise, and do meditation and yoga. It is all helping and finally making me feel peace for a little while. I hope I get good at both of them.

I'm glad Liam is doing well. He has so much strength and

I am so proud to call him my brother. I want to be there to watch his accomplishments. I wish I could fast forward a few months but I know the only way to see the light is to get through the darkness. I miss Chad a lot until I realize there isn't much to miss. I know it's a good thing that I have been alone for a few months because I have always been afraid to be alone because that meant I am always with myself. I never thought people actually loved themselves. I thought it was just bullshit. I never trusted anyone and thought that everyone just wears a mask every day to get through life. I've never been grateful and I didn't realize that. I know now that I have no self-worth, but I'm happy about that because now I can finally deal with the demons, and will finally experience what other people do. I always feel like I can't be loved or feel love but only because I need to learn to love myself. I'm working on overcoming that as well as the trauma with sexual, physical, and mental abuse that happened during all of this as well as self-esteem, depression, and body dysmorphia. I'm telling you all of this because I want you to know that I am making progress finally.

Trish is an amazing therapist. I wish I had seen her sooner but it doesn't matter because now is the right time. Everything happens for a reason and this is the first time I believe that.

Anyways I just wanted you to know although I am struggling, I am finally dealing with things that are keeping me from sobriety. I know that this is finally it. I'm not missing any more holidays or birthdays. Try to have a good holiday. Do it for me! I love you so much! Merry Christmas.

Love,
Your Ladybug

I give in and allow myself to be happy. Online, I compose a post in the Massachusetts Magnolia group, saying that Katie has taken a turn for the better. She sounds good, and I am hopeful. As I go to submit it, my eye catches another post; it's from someone asking for recommendations on sober living. I scan further, reading about people dreading the holidays, those who are missing their children, others in the same dark places I've been in recently, and I wonder if I sound as though I am gloating. No, I decide, there needs to be hope. People recover every day, and we can't lose sight of that. I share my good news, and immediately people offer congratulations and support. People I've never met in my life but who can relate.

Sitting back in my chair, at my desk, I look out the window and see a rabbit finding the last remaining blades of grass, those not covered by the sparse snowfall. I hold Katie's letter close to my heart. Maybe it will be all right after all.

seven

Spring 2016

A few brave crocuses poke through the bare spots, hoping for spring. One day the tree branches are covered with ice; the next it is in the fifties. Today the temperature is promising to reach sixty degrees, and I am taking advantage of it. With Katie safely tucked away among the palm trees of Florida, doing better than she has since the start of this ordeal, I have time to decide what is next for me.

Since moving to Marblehead, I have made a ritual of walking and thinking. Historically significant due to its role in the Revolutionary War, the town boasts several notable sites, including Abbot Hall, which holds the original painting of *The Spirit of '76* and the original deed to Marblehead from a Naumkeag tribe of Native Americans, dated 1684.

Often, I wander up to Old Burial Hill, the town's early burying ground. A memorial obelisk lists the 65 men and boys lost in a great gale on the North Atlantic's Grand Banks in September 1846 that left 43 widows and 155 fatherless children. That storm also effectively ended fishing as Marblehead's principal industry. This town has known misery long before me.

Another route will take me through Old Town and past houses dating back to 1663, each marked by the trade of the owner and the year it was built. Turning down any street changes the story the houses tell, with the names of blacksmiths, merchants, and fisherman proudly displayed—all long gone and certainly having had no idea how significant they would still be hundreds of years later. More than two hundred privately owned colonial homes surround the fishing port and harbor, all adhering to a strict set of regulations where any adjustment has to be approved by the historical committee. (An architect friend calls this group the "hysterical" committee.) The town maintains the look and feel of colonial New England, right down to the cobblestoned streets. The old houses are set so close to the road that in the early evenings you can scarcely avoid peering inside to see how the interiors are decorated. It is hard not to wonder what I did wrong in life that I am standing on the outside looking in, rather than cooking a meal for my family inside of one of these seemingly happy, prosperous homes.

Today, I decide to take a different route: down my street, where every third house is undergoing a renovation, past the bookstore I took the kids to as a reward for a good grade or for their summer reading, farther down, past the small movie theater, which will sell out whenever a new movie comes to town, and past the high school, built in the early 1900s, now redone and housing the middle schoolers. Just before the turn for the elementary school where Katie and Liam both learned to sing "Marblehead Forever," I take a left and go toward the ocean. The homes here are newer, closer to the water, larger. At the beach, a causeway both connects and holds separate the two Marbleheads. On my side of the causeway, the houses and incomes are enviable by most standards, but crossing over the causeway brings the wealth of investment bankers, trust-fund managers, and the Peter Lynches of the world. Yacht clubs and tennis courts are the hub of this small part of town, which is surrounded by water on all sides.

I have given myself the luxury of leaving my phone at home. The phone is now my nemesis. Since Katie's ordeal began, I have been terrified of missing a call and have almost always had my phone in my hand, but now being that connected is torturing me. I have learned enough about this disease that people have begun to come to me for advice and for help. Happy to share anything I know, I've still been going to Matt for anything that I'm unsure about.

The stories coming out of Florida are frightening. There are few regulations and an enormous need, and people with profit on their minds instead of ethics have been inundating the area, opening sober homes and treatment centers that are poorly staffed and often no more than flophouses that bill unsuspecting parents for tens of thousands of dollars. Parents are sending their children there with promises of longer stays in treatment, picturing them recovering in the sunshine they saw advertised on the treatment centers' websites.

Instead, these kids are relapsing and bouncing from one unscrupulous fraudulent hovel to another. Deaths and overdoses in sober homes have been making the news, and although Katie has been fortunate with her stay at Ambrosia and is doing well now at Origins of Hope—an all-female outpatient treatment center and sober living facility with a pool, located in a safe neighborhood and operated by a family who truly cares—I am still scared. I've already had one disappearance in Florida, and the thought that it could happen again is never far from my mind, although Katie is coming up on four months of sobriety.

The bonds developing among the members of the Magnolia Facebook groups are awe-inspiring. People who have never met in person have become one another's support system, often moving on to meeting over coffee and sometimes at funerals. Just recently, one of our Magnolia member's daughters survived an overdose. The mother had heartbreakingly relayed the story of having to take custody of her grandson and section her daughter, Samantha. Another young woman, Amanda, originally from Massachusetts but now in Florida, reached out after overdosing on heroin in a Delray Beach sober house. She had been doing well but found herself in a sober house where her family was being billed for a urinalysis that would have tested positive, although it was actually a meaningless exercise used to bilk the insurance company. As long as the parents paid their bills, no one was ever removed, no matter the test results. After months of encouragement and a call out to Magnolia members, airfare was raised and she came back to Massachusetts, to a treatment facility a town away from her family's home in Haverhill.

The phone has been ringing nonstop, and the text messages and Facebook messages have been overwhelming. The peace of walking along the oceanfront temporarily blots out the stress of so many people in so much pain.

The worst of my problems with Katie seems to be behind me. She is interviewing for jobs and working through the twelve steps. She has new, sober friends and seems happy, so I let myself be happy as well. She still has warrants she needs to clear up, and we decide that once she is stable and has some sober time under her belt, we will approach that next hurdle.

Rhonda, who has already lost one child to heroin, is offered a scholarship for her other child, Kat, for treatment in Recovery Centers of America's new facility in Maryland. Private treatment centers are starting to spring up across Massachusetts as the fear of sending young people out of state rises, and RCA is rumored to be the next to arrive. Kat reluctantly agrees to go, although Rhonda will need to drive her because of her ankle bracelet and the fact that leaving the state will constitute a violation of probation—even though the state offers her too few options for treatment. Going through airport security is not an option. Rhonda's dilemma, as mine was, is: Do I send my child out of state for help and commit a crime or do I let her languish in the same public insurance spin-dry cycle that hasn't worked before? We both choose to take our chances.

I round the corner onto my street, no longer feeling free of stress, and walk in the front door to the sound of my cell phone ringing; the house phone begins to ring as well. I have three texts, and another comes in as I'm looking at my phone. Ignoring the calls, I open a text message from Katie. It's a photo of her taken by a roommate. She is in the living room of her house in Florida. Gail, the owner, has decorated the house with furniture she moved from her own home, and it looks like a place you'd want to live, like a real home. In the forefront of the picture, Katie twirls around in a smart new dress for her second interview at JCPenney. Her hair has grown back in, and she is without sleeves, a sure sign of recovery. I can hear the phone still ringing, but nothing else matters except this, and this moment.

She looks well. That is everything.

Sitting with motorcycle dealers discussing the pros and cons of extended warranty insurance seems like the antithesis of what I do every waking minute, but it pays the bills. There is no reward aside from that. I spend most of my time working on Magnolia, building it, making people aware of the assistance offered, and trying to raise funds. I squeeze in the work that actually pays me, but my heart is not in it—which must be obvious, as my business crawls along without adding any new clients. I force myself to be excited about snowmobile sales and the upcoming spring motorcycle line, and push through the remainder of the meeting.

On my way back from visiting a dealership in Connecticut, I head to my last meeting to see Sammy, who had overdosed over a month ago and who I was able to secure a scholarship for to a treatment center on the Cape. After this I will go home and pack for Florida to visit with Katie tomorrow. I have been counting the days, planning to have a real vacation with her before she starts to work. I bring Sammy a few things to decorate her room and give her the hug I would love to give to my own daughter.

On my way out, I see I've missed several calls from Katie. I get in the car and call her over the Bluetooth.

"Hey, Ladybug."

She is sobbing so hard I can hardly understand her, and my thoughts immediately race, for the first time in months, to relapse. My heart pounds in my chest, and I plead with her to tell me what is wrong.

"They found out about my warrants. I didn't get the job. I'm never going to get a job. I don't even know why I've worked so hard. What's the point? No one is ever going to hire me. I just want to give up."

Katie had been waiting patiently after the second interview with JC Penney and finally called to see when she could start working. The second meeting had gone so well that she'd been introduced to people she would be working alongside and had been spoken to about the company's management training. She had every reason to believe she would have a job, but human resources had run her information and found out that she had outstanding warrants and charges pending for possession of heroin and prostitution. We had been so eager to send her to Florida for treatment when she was willing to go that any thoughts about the future and clearing up those charges had been the least of our problems. Now the past was knocking on her new door.

I calm her down and reassure her that I'll be there tomorrow, and I urge her to hang in there.

"Don't we always figure everything out together?"

She replies with a weak yes and tells me she loves me.

"We'll have fun, sweetie. Don't worry. It will be okay."

As we hang up, it hits me that this is not going to be okay.

I immediately call Gail, the owner of the house, who has spent hours with Katie, helping her practice her interview skills, and ask if she can keep an eye on Katie until I get there. Thoughts of Katie going missing in Florida flood back into my mind, and my lungs practically collapse. I try to distract myself with something pleasant. Still sitting in the car outside the dealership, I remember how Katie and I would sit in the driveway in front of our house listening to a favorite song, just one more time. Listening to music was one of the things that made us so close, and that I miss terribly. I'm scared again. She is right. Any good employer is going to check her past. She can't get a driver's license, and she'll be looking over her shoulder until this is straightened out. And there's only one way to fix it.

As the engine turns over, the radio blasts to life. It startles me, and when I realize what song is playing, the tears roll down my cheeks. It's the Imagine Dragons song, "I Bet My Life," which Katie had mentioned when we met for breakfast at Red's; strung out and hardly able to talk, she had said it reminded her of us.

> "I know I took the path
> That you would never want for me
> I know I let you down, didn't I?"

I put my head down on the steering wheel and hear the words I know she meant for me, the one person she knows will always be there.

"Please forgive me for all I've done."

As the song goes into the refrain I begin to drive and then spend the long ride back from the dealership in Connecticut on the phone, making plans for Katie to move into a nearby sober living house I toured recently. There is no other way. This had to happen sooner or later. As much as I want to freeze time, it looks like she will need to come home. There's no going forward with three open arrest warrants in Massachusetts, and there is certainly no giving up.

In Florida, I pull into the driveway of the ordinary-looking ranch house on a block of identical ranch houses, and no sooner am I out of the car than Katie charges me. Her eyes are sparkling, and her skin is clear—she looks like herself again. She has packed everything she owns, and I've already spoken to Gail. We will have a short vacation in Florida, and then she will fly home with me.

We go to the beach, we go to dinner, we go shopping. She's there, but changed. I chalk it up to nervousness and tell myself I'm imagining things. She introduces me to her housemates, who are all saddened that she will be leaving, albeit proud of her. They have become a makeshift family, all recovering and displaced, clinging to one another, and now they're losing one of their own. With empty promises to keep in touch, Katie throws her bags in the trunk and is ready to go before I have the chance to see most of the house.

The week speeds by, and with two days left in Florida we have run out of distractions and are starting to annoy each other. Out of nervousness, I keep repeating the list of things she needs to do when she gets home, and Katie is tolerating me, barely.

Trying to fill the last two days, I give up on not answering my phone and begin monitoring Facebook, helping people in Massachusetts get into treatment, arranging to hand out Narcan in parking lots and at Narcotics Anonymous meetings. Katie and I pick up a friend she was in treatment with months ago and take him to a grocery store so that he can fill his pregnant girlfriend's refrigerator with healthy food and can go to detox himself, and we then drive him to treatment. Neither of us know what is next, but waiting to leave is driving us both nuts.

"You're making me crazy," Katie says. "I still don't understand why I can't come home, and you keep saying the same thing over and over. You see these things on the sides of my head? They are ears, and they work."

"I know, I can't help myself. Look, see how we're driving each other mad after a week? Once you're back in Massachusetts, you can come over all the time. I promise. Living together is not a good idea. You'd be surrounded by all the people, places, and things that you were when you were using, and I'd be there repeating myself like a lunatic."

We both don't want this to be true, but we know it is. What we really want is to turn back the clock, although neither of us know how far we would need to go back. Maybe you can never go back far enough when you've been dealt the genetic hand that Katie was. We both promise to try to enjoy the rest of the time we have in Florida.

Katie had gone out for a walk when the phone rings; it's Cheryl, a mother who has lost one son and who runs Magnolia's Grief Support page. I let it go to voice mail and it rings again immediately, so I answer.

"Marion's son, Brian, is dead."

"What? What happened? Oh, my God, when?"

"She just found him a few minutes ago. I'm an hour away, but I wanted to see if you could go over, since you're closer. The police are still there, and they haven't taken him out of the house yet."

"Holy shit, Cheryl, I'm in Florida. I'm not coming home for two days. I'll get a flight home sooner. I'm so sorry I'm not there. Is she okay?" I ask, realizing this is a ridiculous question.

"She's upset, but she's holding it together. Her sisters are on their way, too."

"I'm going to call her. I'll call you back."

It's too close. Much too close. Brian had been doing so well when he had a slipup. Marion went right to work finding him help, and he was going to enter treatment after the weekend. I can't even imagine what she is going through, but I have to call her. I'm not sure if I would have done that a year or so ago, but if I have learned anything from how I was treated when Katie was arrested, it's that it is best to err on the side of reaching out.

Marion answers on the second ring. She is crying but calm.

"Marion, I don't know what to say."

"We were going to watch the game today, like we always do, and he was still asleep, so I went upstairs, and when he didn't answer the door, I went in and shook his foot. I knew he was gone as soon as I saw him. I called the police, then Cheryl."

The enormous pain of finding your child dead in his bed is beyond comprehension. They had been buddies, and she was always his biggest champion. They followed all the sports teams together. Basketball, baseball, football. The Red Sox played the Blue Jays today. It was the fifth game of the season. The game began at 1:07 p.m. The Sox lost 3–0. Brian would've been dead for over twelve hours by the time it started.

"He's still upstairs, Maureen."

"I'd be right over, but I'm in Florida. I'm coming home early, though. I'll call you later to check in on you and then again when I get home. I love you, sweetie. I'm so very sorry."

"Thank you. I'll see you soon."

I'm sitting on the couch staring into space when Katie comes in from outside. She immediately senses that all the air has left the room and asks me what's wrong.

Sweet Marion, who has helped me from the start, who had written to Katie in Florida, offering words of encouragement although she had never met her, and had sent her a bracelet with "Never give up hope" written on it so she would know she was being thought of, had lost her only child. We both know that it could have just as easily been Katie. She sits next to me, wrapped in my arms, and neither of us say a word. There is nothing to say.

The wake is brutal. It isn't the first funeral for a child who was a member of our group, but for me it is the most personal. Poor Marion looks small and broken in the receiving line; I want to make it all go away for her. An endless stream of people who loved Brian and still love Marion file past. He was so handsome, so young. No words can say enough, so I hug her and tell her I love her.

I stand for a while with Rhonda, who knows the pain of a life cut short all too well. She lost her youngest daughter, Mariah, in 2011, and you can see the pain that never goes away written across her face. People standing in the overflow room hug and exchange pleasantries, trying to forget for a second why they are there. Then reality will hit: the fear of whose child will be next, and the knowledge that with thousands of children dying, there will be another grieving mother and, soon, another. It feels all too familiar. I make sure to take a Mass card as I leave and put it inside my wallet. I promise myself that if I get tired or discouraged, I will look at that card and do what needs to be done in honor of Brian and Mariah.

In the early 1980s, with two small children, I worked as a waitress in Forest Hills, Queens, and spent any free time I could manage to scrounge for myself hanging out and being twenty in Greenwich Village. Thirty-plus years ago, the Village was still one of the few places where it was safe to be openly gay, but Forest Hills was also progressive, and most of the people I worked with in the bars and restaurants there were gay men. On the weekends my children spent with their grandmother or father, I worked during the days and finished up around midnight, because no one in New York went anywhere before midnight anyhow. The West Village was mostly gay, and the East Village was mostly punk, and all of this was twenty minutes and a world away from where I lived in Queens, a young mother struggling to support two young children.

When I hung out there, with those fresh-faced boys, experiencing freedom for the first time, all of us tired and wanting to laugh after a night of catering to others, I found the most definite expression of being exactly who you are without judgment. No one was asked to accept anyone's lifestyle or differences because no one judged in the first place. It was getting easier to be gay in the world, at least there in the Village. This was all true until people started to die.

It happened slowly, and then with such speed it seemed as though no one was safe. The speed of the deaths took your breath away. One minute a person was working alongside you, and the next moment they were gone. If someone lost a little weight, you'd wonder; if they missed work, you would plan for a funeral.

Richie was my friend. He was openly gay and didn't care who knew it, and he spoke up when a joke was made at his expense. He was comfortable in his own skin and fearless. He was in a long-term relationship, and we'd share war stories about how hard it was to live with a man. They were annoying, inconsiderate, and they cheated. Why he saw himself as someone above the "man" label I'm not sure, but he did.

When I ran into him one day, he told me that his partner was sick. I could see the knowledge of impending doom in his face. It was now a time of fear. The mid-1980s brought a lot of questions and fewer answers. Richie had reason to be afraid. In a matter of weeks, his partner was dead. Within months, Richie was dead, too.

I sometimes feel like I am reliving that time. The losses we are experiencing every day of young, otherwise healthy people who should be beginning long, productive lives feels very familiar. Once again, we find ourselves looking for signs in the people we love, studying a crowd of people and wondering who is next.

Even in those early years, with the fear that surrounded AIDS, coupled with the stigma and prejudice associated with being gay, the obvious answer was to stop the secrecy and shaming by educating ourselves and the public. The evolution of treating AIDS like any other disease and the openness and acceptance that the LGBT community is only now beginning to experience can be traced directly back to those who understood that shame and stigma kill. The people I knew and the people who were at the forefront of working with those with AIDS recognized that silence equaled death.

I can't stop thinking that we will look back at this time in a similar way, and I only hope that an understanding of substance use disorder as a disease will help eliminate or at least reduce the shame and stigma associated with it, allowing more people to get help. And I hope that those loved ones supporting a person who is suffering will come out of the shadows to heal the family, too. It has to start somewhere.

The morning after Brian's funeral, after watching my dear friend bury her only child, I am alarmed by a posting about a skit on *Saturday Night Live* the previous evening. The show's parody on the heroin epidemic portrays families who use Heroin AM to wake up and Cocaine PM to go to sleep. I am horrified. My first thought is for Marion. What if she sees this? Is *SNL* that desperate for material? Does anyone really find humor in this?

During the AIDS epidemic, many were afraid to reach out and refused treatment, but everything turned around when people started to speak up. So, I write my outrage.

It is seven days since Brian's death, and I cannot hold it in. I write to get the anger out, but then I realize that just putting my feelings down is not enough. The people at *SNL* need to know they are wrong. They need to apologize for making light of the death of my friend's son.

I post my rant on Magnolia's open page, and I hit a nerve. It's incredible. All the people quietly accepting that they are the butt of the joke copy and share my letter. I send it to *SNL* but receive no response. The response comes instead from mothers. I see my words on the Facebook pages of people I have never met and of groups across the country. The local newspaper calls and asks for my opinion; then the *Boston Globe*, the *Washington Post*, and media outlets from across the country copy a paragraph and, most importantly, provide a hyperlink to our website. Hundreds of people find us and join.

I would think after the loss of John Belushi, Chris Farley and other beloved members of your cast that you would have realized that heroin addiction is about as funny as genocide, but judging by your show last night I'd have to say, apparently not. You have just attempted to make a serious health epidemic into a joke and it is nothing less than disgusting. Apologize and make it right.

In CNN's story, Chris Farley's brother Tom Farley Jr. is quoted directly below my paragraph. He says that he is disappointed and saddened. I remain furious. CNN calls. My letter is included in an article on its website, and its producers invite us to be part of a show on the heroin epidemic that will be broadcast live on *Anderson Cooper 360°*.

I call Rhonda.

"You're not going to believe this. CNN just called and invited us on the Anderson Cooper show. Do you want to go?"

"Ahh, hell yes, I want to go!"

It's too soon for Marion, but Cheryl takes the third spot. Rhonda, Cheryl, and I drive to the CNN studios and meet a New York Magnolia member named Debbie who had helped to arrange the invitation. Soon we are all watching the membership numbers tick upward.

We are being heard. Finally, someone is listening.

eight | Summer 2016

There are Katie spottings everywhere. What started so hopefully as a safe stay in a sober living house in Massachusetts, just a few short miles from home, has turned into another disappearing act. Her friends who care about her reach out and tell me where they think she might be found. It's when people I don't even know get in touch with me on Facebook to tell me stories of what is happening with her that I begin to go just a little crazy. She continues to check in. I track her on the phone to towns but not addresses. She makes calls to Chelmsford from Salem, and an hour later calls from Lawrence back to Lynn. She seems to be constantly on the move. I contact Gabe Wright, who lies and tells me he doesn't know where she is, and then finally he disappears as well.

I am back where I started, but now I understand so much more. The things I've learned terrify me. Children can be alive one minute, gone the next. Everyone I know seems to have lost a child. I live among the walking wounded and fight against my turn.

A friend tells me that Katie has been spotted two towns over, describes the car she was in and the people she was with. I call Mike and tell him to come over right away.

"What's your plan, Inspector Gadget?"

"I don't have one," I answer as I put the back seats flat in the RAV4.

He gets in the passenger side, and we drive out of Marblehead and through Salem, past the building of the arrest. When I see the number 250 painted across the dirty glass door, my stomach turns, as it always does. I explain to Mike how I know where she is, or *about* where she is, and tell him to keep an eye out for her.

We get to the general area where she was spotted. I learned that she is staying in some fleabag hotel known for drug use and prostitution and is out looking for more drugs. We circle the parking lot, but she is nowhere to be seen.

"How exactly do you expect to find her?" Mike asks.

"I don't know, but lacking any ideas from you, I think you'll have to leave it to me, don't you?"

"Okay, wiseass, I'm almost afraid to ask, but what's your plan when and if we find her?"

"I just want to talk to her. That's all. I want to see her with my own eyes. So quit your yapping and keep your eyes peeled!"

We both know I'm lying.

I've had numerous friends of Katie's tell me how bad she looks—far too thin and out of control. Whoever coined the phrase *heroin chic* should be smacked. How can Katie have come so far and let it all go? How fucking stupid was I to think this was over? She is back to only texting, so that we don't hear the hoarseness in her voice, the slurring of her speech. Not a day passes where I don't get a message saying that she loves me.

"I see her!" Mike yells, hanging half out of the passenger-side window.

"Keep your bald head down, for God's sake, and stop shouting!"

He sucks his head back into the car and slinks down, keeping an eye on her.

"Just drive, Gadget, and remember who saw her first," he jokes. "Thank God we can still laugh."

I agree. And then the laughing is over.

I speed up. There she is, sitting in the back seat of a beat-up Toyota Corolla, with another girl in the front and a young guy in the driver's seat. Obviously having seen too many episodes of *CSI*, I screech into the parking lot and block the Corolla from moving by parking sideways behind it. I jump out and race over to the side of the car closest to Katie before any of them fully figure out what is happening. Katie is in fact shooting up, needle in hand. That horror registers only hours later. In the moment, she sees me and automatically smiles, her arm still tied off, not realizing what's going on and only knowing that she sees "Mom." I lift her out of the car and half-carry, half-push her to the door of the RAV4. The needle and drugs fall.

Over my shoulder, I am screaming, "Mike, for the love of God, get in the fucking car!" He is bellowing in the face of the kid in the driver's seat, having no idea what he is trying to accomplish aside from possibly making the kid wet his pants. By this time, we have become a spectacle. I continue to shout at Mike to get in the fucking car.

Katie, high as a kite, doesn't begin to fight until I throw her into the back of the RAV4, which now is a long open bed instead of seats, giving evidence to the plan I had all along. I easily get her in and then jump on top of her, slamming the door behind myself.

I hear people behind me finally come to life, screaming, "Leave them alone," and I assume they are yelling at Mike as the driver's-side back door opens. Katie is pulling in that direction as the girl I saw in the front seat sticks her cell phone in the car and starts talking like she is Katie's lawyer. Tall, thin, and mousy, she wears glasses that look too large for her face. Without any knowledge of the situation, you could imagine this girl in a library studying for an advanced calculus exam. Instead, she is filming me wrestling with my daughter in the back of my car and is loudly informing me that she has called the police.

"Shut the fucking door before I let her go and kick the shit out of you!"

She continues to stick herself and the phone, which is now certainly recording my complete and long-awaited nervous breakdown, into the rear side door of the SUV. As she moves in to get a better view, I hold Katie down with the left side of my body and my left hand; with my right, I reach for the girl's throat, or the camera, or both.

I scream to Mike, "Get in the fucking car, Michael!" The crowd has grown, and I realize that the people gathering around are shouting at the idiot holding the door open and videotaping. They are telling her to back off and yelling, "It's their daughter. Get away from them and let them take her!"

"You realize that if she gets away because of you," I warn the skinny girl, "I'll be free to go after you, right?" Reality hits her stoned, formerly expressionless face, and she finally lets go of the door. I pull it shut just as Mike gets behind the wheel.

"Drive! Drive! Let's get the fuck out of here," I scream, while using all of my strength to hold Katie down. Her eyes are now wild, and she is fighting as only a ninety-pound heroin addict can—with the strength of ten men.

We pull out of the parking lot to applause, and I can't believe that this is my life.

"Where are we going?" Mike asks.

"Are you fucking kidding me?" I say, as Katie and I are caught in the battle of our lives. I am now trying to make sure she doesn't get out of the car while it's moving, having just wrestled the door handle from her. "I don't fucking know. Head to Gloucester. Maybe we can get someone at the Gloucester Police Department to help us."

We drive through peaceful neighborhoods, passing children at play, families barbecuing, a large woman with a small child wearing heart-shaped sunglasses. We are any other family driving on a Sunday in their family-friendly SUV, except in this suburban vehicle my daughter has just bit me in an effort to escape.

"You bit me. You little brat. I think you broke the skin."

We both look at my arm, shocked.

"Mommy, I'm so sorry."

For a moment, she is Katie again. Katie, who would never hurt me, or do drugs, or forget to say good night. Her eyes well up, and I relax my grip on her; the wildness returns like flash paper igniting, and we are back at it.

I manage to get my weight back on her—me and Ben and Jerry—and she finally gives up a little. I'm still afraid that she will open the door and jump out onto Route 128, so I continue to hold her as we pull off the highway and enter downtown Gloucester. Catching my breath, I lean down and kiss her on the top of the head.

I pray that someone I know in the Angel Program will be able to help. The Angel Program was designed to help instead of punish: you can bring anyone in need of treatment for a substance use disorder to the police station, where they will be paired with an "Angel," who will make sure they get into treatment. Several officers from the police department—in particular, Jeremiah Nicastro—support the program fully, as does Gloucester's mayor, Sefatia Romeo Theken. One small department is changing the face of how law enforcement deals with those needing treatment. PAARI, or the Police Assisted Addiction and Recovery Initiative, was born out of this program.

I sincerely doubt, however, that bringing someone into the station kicking and screaming falls under the auspices of the program. Nevertheless, I tell Mike to keep going, because I have no idea what else to do. The thought that I may have actually lost my mind occurs to me more than once. I have just kidnapped a person. I loosen my grip on her as we begin to drive through Gloucester.

"If I let you go," I ask Katie, "can we sit here and just talk for a minute?

"Let me go, like, let me out of the car?"

"Yes, but first we need to talk."

Mike looks at me and shakes his head. He can't believe what has just transpired or the fact that it may all be for nothing. He doesn't even have to say anything for me to know what he is thinking.

Katie and I are both sitting cross-legged in the back of the car. I'm rubbing the spot on my arm that she bit, where an angry mouth-shaped welt is turning purple, and I look over and see the pain it causes her in her eyes.

"Katie, you know how much we love you, right?"

"Yes, I know, but you can't control me, you can't rip me out of cars and embarrass me in front of my friends."

"I know, I know. That was wrong, but it felt like the only thing we could do. We are afraid, afraid of you getting hurt, arrested, or dying. Did you just see that gang out in Lowell, the Kilby Street Gang, that held all those women who were addicted to heroin and forced them to prostitute themselves and wouldn't let them leave? That could be you. Don't you understand that you're killing yourself?"

"It was Worcester, Mom, and it's you who doesn't understand. I'd rather be dead than living like this. I stay alive, force myself through another detox, go to treatment I don't want to be in, and hold myself back from doing the shot that's just a little too much and would kill me because I love you, too." Crying now, she adds, "I can't stop. I try and I can't. I see other people who want to be sober, and I just can't make myself want it enough. If there were a way for me to just end this all without hurting you I would, but you just never give up on me. Why don't you give up?"

"That's the one thing I will never do, honey. Never."

"Can I get out of the car now?" she says, quickly glancing in the rearview mirror to adjust her makeup.

I look at Mike and then back at her. "Okay. I love you."

"I love you both."

We watch her walk away, take the phone out of her purse, and immediately start texting. We are beaten, not by her or this insanity that just occurred, but by the realization that there is nothing we can do.

When things start to feel wrong, with that unmistakable gnawing sense that something just isn't right, I convince myself that I am imagining things. As the murmur grows louder, it isn't the slow pulling away, the inability to find a job or follow up on anything, or the fact that Katie is always busy but never seems to do anything she can share. It takes her leaving all of her belongings in the sober house I've once again paid for and disappearing into thin air, like a ghost. I have coaxed myself to believe, to want, to feel gratitude, to think it's possible that the worst of it might be over. You'd assume this would get easier, but it doesn't. In fact, each time I convince myself it's safe to have hope, the cliff I fall off feels higher and higher, and the crawl up the mountainside gets just a little more difficult.

The reason the groups are so helpful is that the connection to people we know and love becomes so strained; there is no way to imagine how horrific it is unless you are going through it.

One morning Joan calls me. She often checks in: to run an idea, a new problem, or sometimes the same old problem disguised as a new problem by me. I try to give the decision back to her, as I always do whenever anyone asks me what they should do; they'll have to live with whatever happens afterward. It may sound like a cop-out, but it's not. I know what the books say and I know what the experts will tell me, but I also know that at the end of the day, I've had to live with the possibilities each time I've made a decision related to Katie. So I can only talk from my own experience and share what I have found works for me. Every situation is unique.

Joan's son, Christopher, wants to come home, and she wants me to tell her what to do. He is promising to go to detox, but he wants to stay at home for a few days first. If Joan lets him do that, he will go, or so he says. I listen, and although I know what I would do and I believe she knows what she should do, I can't possibly make this decision for her.

"I want him home in his own bed, under my roof, where I can protect him until he goes. I'm afraid if I say no, he will never go," she tells me in between sobs.

"How do you feel about him using in your house?" I ask.

"I've already told him that is absolutely not happening."

"Joan, I think unless the goal is for him to go to detox very quickly, he will need to use in order not to be sick, based on what you've told me about his current drug use."

Okay, I think, *I haven't crossed the line between telling her what to do and educating her.*

"I know you're right. I guess the idea of him coming home, where he belongs, is just so tempting. I think what I really want is my little boy from ten years ago home, maybe not the person he is right now. I want to go back in time and start over. I just wish I had known you and all of what I know now back then."

Joan has hit the nail on the head. I wonder, not for the first time, how far I would go back to change the course of events that led to my current reality. I hear her sniffling, choking back tears.

"I can't and would never tell you what to do," I say, "because whatever you decide, we both know it could all go horribly wrong. There's no instruction booklet or blueprint for this, along with most of the things we do as mothers. Keep in mind that I know all that I do now and still make huge mistakes because my emotions get in the way. You can't intellectualize your responses when it comes to love for a child. I can tell you what to do based on research and still do the exact opposite myself, and it might just work. You can only inform yourself and then go with your gut. Ultimately, you need to live with that decision, so you have to be comfortable with it."

"You know I was hoping you'd tell me not to let Christopher come home?"

"You might want to ask yourself if you weren't hoping that because it would affirm what you already know. I think it's real progress that he wants to come home and he is willing to talk about going to treatment. Just a year or so ago, when we first started talking, you couldn't even find him. Think about the progress. He knows you love him and he's coming to you now. I suggest you define your boundaries and stick with them, whatever you decide. I know it's not where you want it to be, but this is all a big step in the right direction, don't you think?"

"Yes," she agrees, "I guess it is. I've stopped helping him, bailing him out, and thinking this was something that would pass if I hid it."

"I really think he is starting to take responsibility if he is suggesting detox."

I try to comfort her without losing sight of the fact that Christopher is likely manipulating her. A year ago, Joan would've opened the doors, given him back his car keys, paid for a lawyer for the latest arrest, and offered to replace the clothes he'd lost on the last run, all because he was telling her that he would agree to go to a treatment program, which she would also need to pay for. She had run through all her savings and a home equity loan by the time he turned twenty-one. He's twenty-six now and on MassHealth, so it will be a process getting him into detox. My concern for Joan is that she will let him in and he will overdose, using at home, alone, in his own bed, or that in the short time he is there, he will steal everything he didn't steal the last time he was home.

"Why don't you tell him to call me?" I suggest. "Let's take it out of your hands, and I'll work with him on finding a detox bed. Let's see how serious he is."

I answer the phone over and over during the day, and none of the calls are from Christopher. Joan calls me around seven that evening to ask the question she already knows the answer to: if I have heard from her son. I tell her I have not.

"Just because he hasn't called today doesn't mean he won't," I remind her. "We are always planting seeds."

She asks me to call him, but I can't. If he can't even make the call to me, then he won't follow through; that much I understand.

"I just don't know what I did wrong," she tells me. "I still can't stop asking myself that question."

I can relate to what she says. I did it, too. I know that I raised all four children the same way, by the same rules, making the same mistakes and providing the same amount of love, but they are all vastly different and have their own personalities and inherited their own propensity for addiction when they were born. I look at my own life and how I was raised, and if ever someone should have been the one to try to solve problems by abusing drugs and alcohol, it should have been me—yet I could always say "enough." It doesn't make sense, even with all I've learned.

What could I have done differently? I have come to the conclusion that there may not be an answer to that, and that I, despite the endless amount of love I have for my daughter, am not more powerful than a disease.

The phone continues to ring all evening. If I ever wanted to have more children, I have them now: an extended family of kids that I've helped get into treatment, and then those who my name got passed on to, and the friends who often reach out on their behalf. It grows every day. Some of them have burned their own families out, a few never had strong family connections at all, but many just feel too guilty about all the things they have done to talk to their own families, so they reach out to me.

Many of Katie's friends keep in touch with me, too. The old friends she grew up with check in to see how she's doing, and some of the newer friends she's been in treatment with will call to let me know that they've seen her and that she's their version of okay. So, when the phone rings one morning and it's Pete, he could either be putting me in touch with someone who needs help or sharing some news he hopes will protect Katie. This time he is reaching out about Susanna.

"I have this friend, she testified against the Kilby Street Gang in Worcester and the district attorney's office was going to help her, but she ran because she was scared. She's in trouble, big trouble. She needs to go now. Can I tell her to call you?"

"Where is she?"

"At a motel in Danvers."

"Give her my number, and I'll make a few phone calls. She is really going to go to detox, right?"

"Yes, definitely, but she'll need a ride."

What the fuck, I say to myself. I had a day planned, but this is more important. I know the place he's speaking about: a run-down two-story motel stuck off the side of the road, behind an equally run-down Denny's. The motel is full of transient sorts of people: those who were recently evicted, people cheating on their spouses, some "telly" parties for those who don't have a home in which to do drugs, and prostitutes.

Susanna calls, and she sounds serious. I can't put my finger on what creates that impression, but anyone who has worked with people who have a substance use disorder will know exactly what I mean. Somehow the person's voice will convey a sense of resignation and an urgency, the commitment to do whatever they need to do to get off the roller coaster.

There is a series of questions I run through when someone comes to me for help. Unfortunately, the first one after asking them if they are "safe" at the moment—a sort of rhetorical question, since most people reaching out haven't been "safe" in a very long time—is about their insurance. In Massachusetts, we are incredibly lucky to have a comparatively robust state insurance plan called MassHealth. In most states across the country, the residents are not so lucky. There are a multitude of services and detox and treatment programs offered to those covered by MassHealth, all of which usually work off a waiting list. The better the program, the longer the wait. Private insurance makes it much easier and the choices more appealing, though the true measure of a treatment center is not whether there are 300-count cotton sheets and a salad bar but, rather, the quality of the program and the dedication of the staff. I have my list of places I know to be good and would normally start at the top, where I am relatively sure that detox will lead to a twenty-one-day program and then, hopefully, to more longer-term treatment. But from what I've been told about Susanna's situation, there isn't time for that. I ask if she is ready to leave right now, and she says she is. Good sign. I get the room number and tell her I'm on my way.

Most detox centers will know who is being discharged that day first thing in the morning, around eight or eight-thirty. That's when you want to make a call for someone: they can go in right away and will be guaranteed a bed for the night. But right now, it's one p.m., which is also too late to try to land a spot before the second wave of discharges, which happens around noon. I know I need to get Susanna into detox right now or else she could be dead tomorrow. So, I call up a detox center that is not my favorite, knowing they will have a bed, because few people with any other options would want to go there. It'll do.

There are way too many cars in the motel's parking lot in the middle of this steamy, warm day. I wonder what's going on behind all those closed doors and realize I don't want to know. When I knock, a petite young woman with gigantic brown eyes that remind me of Katie's opens the door. Her hair is in a towel, and another towel is wrapped around her. I'll have to go in. She is midway through applying her makeup, which she does with such expertise I'm not surprised to learn she went to school for cosmetology.

"Thank you so much for helping me," she says, as she rushes around the cramped room, which looks as though she has been there forever and never let the cleaners in. "I'm so sorry the room is such a mess."

There are two queen beds, and both are unmade. She doesn't know just how many messes I have seen, how many sheetless mattresses, blood-splattered from too many failed attempts at a vein, smelling of sweat and drugs and hopelessness.

It's the sort of room where all the pictures and lamps are bolted to the walls or the furniture, as if someone would want to take them. I sit on the edge of the less rumpled bed and notice a pair of men's work boots in the corner. I smarten up then and stand near the door, asking Susanna if there is anyone else here.

She's either high or nervous or both and talks in a clipped manner, quickly, and mostly without looking at me.

"No, he's at work. He's an electrician. Good guy. He let me stay with him. No funny business, just a friend."

I relax a little and sit on the edge of the bed again. The door is open, and nothing that could fly in is any worse than what is already in the room, so I leave it that way. The room reeks and is brutally hot and still.

There are empty beer bottles and clothes everywhere. A tray with used needles, cotton pulled off Q-tips, a bottle cap, an opened water bottle, and some matches are on the bedside. Six or seven green trash bags line the wall, full of what I am told are clothes and everything Susanna has in the world.

"They are never going to let me take everything in with me. I'm so sick of losing things."

Katie has lost everything she has owned. More than twice. She insisted on taking everything when she moved in with Chad; then little by little she went from place to place with only what she could carry. I've begun to hold on to things for people entering rehab. The thought of them losing the small amount of possessions they have managed to hold on to makes me sick. My garage looks a bit like the Salvation Army.

"I can keep your things at my house. Just pack up what you'll need for a week or two. You can do laundry there, and when you're out and we get you somewhere safe to live, I'll pick you up and give you everything back."

Susanna eyes me suspiciously.

"I do it for a lot of people. Trust me. I'll give it back. I definitely don't want your stuff."

Not really having a choice, she packs two plastic tote bags with what she will need and puts her makeup case aside.

"Why are you doing this for me?" she asks as we're heading to my car.

"Because you need help and I know how to help you."

As I drive, she talks a little about the children who have been taken away, about the car accident that started her serious addiction to pain-killers, and of the drug-using mother who raised her.

"I think back now about how my mom and three friends would go to the bathroom together in our house. I didn't know what they were doing then, but I get it now. There were just always drugs, so when I was about thirteen and they offered me some, it didn't seem like a big deal. Your daughter is lucky to have you as her mom."

"You can borrow me. Trust me, I think my daughter would tell you that there is more than enough of me to go around!"

We both laugh and it cuts the tension, and we enter the empty parking lot of the detox center, get out, and open the front door, which leads directly to the waiting room. Once again, I am struck by the misery of the hard, plastic chairs and the despair in the air. It smells like a hospital, full of disinfectant. A boy, alone and no more than twenty, sits in the far corner vomiting into a garbage pail.

A woman walks in and makes a beeline to the reception desk, careful not to allow eye contact with anyone. I can hear her say she is delivering clothes and cigarettes for her daughter Olivia Rose. I think of the love and excitement involved in giving a baby such a sweet name. Nowhere in the plans were deliveries to seedy detox centers. Another woman, in her thirties, sits alone, perspiring and staring at the clock.

Susanna is sweet and normal and wanted a different life, just like Katie. Her family situation was nothing like ours, but somehow they have wound up in the same situation. The nurse calls her name, and she asks if I can come with her. This is good-bye. Susanna gathers her bags, as well as the pens and adult coloring books I bought for her earlier. She gives me a big hug, and I can feel the ribs in her back through her shirt, just like I have with Katie.

"You're going to be okay," I assure her. "They will ask you if you want to sign a release so that the case managers can talk to someone about your discharge plan. Put me on your release and call me. I can't help you if you don't call me, okay?"

"I'll call, I promise."

I stand there for a moment, thanking God for allowing me to be a part of her journey and praying that she will find the strength to get well. I am not going to give up on her any more than I am giving up on Katie. Someone has to make it; I see it happen every day. Why can't it be both of them? I shake off the thoughts about those who don't survive and go to the reception desk. Olivia Rose's mom, wearing the same hopeless expression, still standing there filling out a form, looks up at me.

"It's not easy, is it?" she says, assuming I am Susanna's mother.

"No, it's not, not ever," I reply. "Listen, I don't know if you have any support, but I run a peer support group online called Magnolia New Beginnings. I have these cards with the website on it. It's all free, and basically, it's like a parents meeting on Facebook. You join the closed group, and no one aside from members can see anything you post. It's all peer advice, so you don't have to worry about someone selling you anything; it's just an incredible source of support and information. The other members know the answers because they have been through it all. We have groups all over the United States, and there's a ton of files with information in them, too. You're not alone, and you shouldn't have to feel alone."

By now both Olivia Rose's mom and the receptionists, clearly someone else's moms, are teary. I leave the postcards at the desk and encourage them to pass them on. By that evening, Magnolia has nineteen additional members.

I bring Susanna's clothes home, and after a couple loads of laundry, I fold them neatly and put them into new heavy-duty plastic tote bags, never forgetting that she may need to carry them with her again. I place them next to a young man from Maryland's belongings and slightly apart from Katie's suitcase and the bags she couldn't carry anymore. I sit in a stray beach chair and survey the garage.

In the corner are two snowboards Katie and Liam have outgrown, propped lazily against the wall; bicycle pumps hang from hooks, with their hoses reaching down toward the long-abandoned bikes; a wooden shelf looks like a who's who of balls, one from every conceivable type of sport. The remnants of childhoods played out in this garage. Turning my head toward the door, I recall a summer day much like today over ten years prior, the cool of the garage a refuge from the heat and August humidity.

Katie played the bass and sang background in a band. They wrote original music and did covers of a variety of pissed-off bands, like the Ramones, AC/DC, and Green Day. They were good, even great, for their age. It always seemed to embarrass her that she did this, and she never thought she was very talented. Much like the day she sang the solo in church, she showed no nervousness in front of the crowd.

They played school shows, then competitions against other high school bands, then concerts organized to show off young talent. At first it was fun, and then a mother who believed she was raising the next big pop star inserted herself into the band by playing agent to the stars, ending all the fun and alienating the parents.

Katie decided that she did not want to be in a band controlled by the girl's mother and told her so, although she felt obligated to perform somewhere they had already been booked. A huge Fourth of July show was planned in Marblehead at Crocker Park, a beautiful venue where concerts were held for days that holiday weekend. It was an honor and an obligation. Nevertheless, the vocalist and her mother had taken their rehearsal studio with them. We switched the practice venue to my garage, and the neighbors good-naturedly tolerated the tryouts for a new lead singer—some of which were brutal—and the rehearsals. Even with the new addition, all the members were going to have to take a turn up front. Katie didn't want to sing in front of everyone. I didn't understand. I still don't. So, one evening we went downstairs and turned on the equipment and the microphone. We'd brought down a CD player, and I put on the song she was scheduled to sing.

"I can't do it," she said.

"But you've been taking vocal lessons along with the bass lessons for months, and you have a beautiful voice."

"The more I think about singing alone, the more I know I won't be able to do it."

"Then stop thinking about it and just do it, here, with me. Instead of thinking about it, just do it. We can do it together."

Even alone in the garage, I knew exactly how she must have felt now that I'd agreed to sing with her, our audience only the lawn mower and weed whacker. I turned on the music, and several times we needed to start over because neither of us could stop laughing. The introduction would begin, and by the time we were at the part where we should join in and sing, I had made one too many rock-and-roll faces and we'd both be bent over giggling.

"Okay, let's be serious."

The serious faces made us laugh. We were hopeless.

I started the music again, and we both leaned toward the microphone and right on cue began to sing over the TobyMac coming from the CD player.

"She said she's had enough . . ."

I started to step back and let her take it on her own, which sounded so much better. The struggle to sing the words on their own was foreboding, but I couldn't have known that then.

"They say you never know what you got till it's gone
(Never know what you got till it's gone)"

I pulled away, as if my hands were leaving her body as she swam on her own for the first time. I could see the nervousness subside, and she started to sway as she sang. When she picked up the bass to play along and started the CD for the fifth or sixth time, I knew she would be okay. We did it.

As I sit in the empty garage now, next to Katie's abandoned belongings, I would do anything to help her through the trouble she's in. I ask myself, first silently and then screaming at the walls, "How much fucking worse, God, how much worse is this going to get?" I sob, "Please don't take my girl. Please!"

'm going to meet Eric," says Mike, who rarely opens a call with hello and instead vomits whatever he has to say.

"That's so nice for you. Who is Eric, and why does it always sound like you're calling from inside a jet turbine?"

"I'm working my second job in the machine shop. Eric is where she went after fighting with Bob."

"She's not living with Bob the scumbag anymore? Where did she meet Eric? In the same mystery meeting she met Bob?"

Although this guy Bob has Mike fooled into thinking he is helping her, I don't believe it. Mike has told me Bob looks harmless—fat, short, and over fifty-five. Bob owns a small auto body shop that rarely seems to do any auto body work. A friend of Katie's had told me two nights ago that she had messaged him asking for money from the address of the house Bob owned. The friend was waiting outside for Katie, and the police told him to move on because it was a house known for drugs.

I put the phone on speaker and start scrubbing the sink—not because it's dirty but because I need to do something with my hands.

"Why do you hate that guy so much?" he asks. "She introduced him to me, and they both said they met at an AA meeting. He is renting her a room in exchange for her doing some paperwork for his company. He's got another kid there doing the same thing."

"There's something wrong with the whole thing. It doesn't feel right, and I think she's lying. Please, she's using again, even though she says she is not. I can tell by all the texts and the lack of conversation. Plus, I haven't seen her and her arms, which always means the same thing."

"Okay, when I see Eric, I'll take a look at her arms. Do you want to come?"

"No, I don't. Just get the address."

"It's off the Salem Common."

"Oh, good luck with that!"

According to Mike, Eric is a slightly younger, more hippie version of Bob. Eric is doing Katie a favor by letting her stay with him, and he has promised to keep her safe. It makes no sense to me why this person would do a favor for a complete stranger and ask for nothing in return. Probably because it isn't true. He plays music and makes food out of medical marijuana as an occupation. Mike finds out she bounces between there and Bob's house for some weeks. And then, not long after her birthday, she agrees to meet.

I recall last year's birthday in Florida, out of her mind on what I had later found out was flakka, a popular synthetic drug in Florida, initially presumed to have caused a young man to have a psychotic episode so severe he attacked a couple sitting in their garage and ate most of the man's face. He killed them both, and it seemed like something that could be attributed to that awful new drug. Katie is appearing progressively worse, but I tell myself she is okay and decide to try to be grateful that she is with me.

She stays the night, and as we do errands the following day, I watch her decline slowly, then more quickly. Sweating with the air conditioner on and shivering in the heat. Developing a runny nose and cold-like symptoms. She's getting annoyed by everything we planned to do and finally asks me to drop her off at a convenience store.

"Are you going to Gabe's house?"

"He doesn't even live there anymore, Mom."

Her tone is that of the teenage girl she once was.

"Bob has an appointment with his lawyer and he is still there, so he said he'd give me a ride."

"Bob does not have a meeting that lasted all day with a lawyer on a Sunday, and you have a ride and you're looking at her."

"Are you kidnapping me again?"

"Okay, okay. I'll drop you off."

I bring her to a store around the corner from a local college. She says she needs cigarettes, which I will not buy for her. I watch her walk in and, as I do each time she walks away, I wonder if I will ever see her again. I quickly text her that I love her, just in case. She responds that she loves me, too.

Less than twenty-four hours later, I get a call from Mike. A friend at the Salem Police Department told him that they had just picked up Katie in an ambulance, around the corner from where I dropped her off the day before. Someone had come home to their apartment building from work and found her on the landing of the stairs, which she had apparently fallen down after overdosing. Whoever she was with had left her for dead, crumpled and blue, at the bottom of the staircase like a bag of garbage. It took four shots of Narcan and CPR to revive her, and she is on her way to the hospital.

By the time he calls me, he is almost at the ER.

I am putting my shoes on.

"Wait a minute. You're not going to believe this shit. She is standing *outside* the hospital."

"What the fuck? That can't be her!"

I can hear Mike calling for her out the car window and her voice, annoyed, asking him why he is there.

"Katie! For Christ's sake, you just overdosed and almost died. What are you doing standing outside?"

"I'm fine. I'm waiting for a ride, and I'm not going with you."

"That's the last straw. You may not be coming with me today, but

I'm sectioning you tomorrow morning. Do you hear that? I'm fucking done with this."

"Fuck you!" I hear her screaming at him while walking away.

"I probably shouldn't have said that," Mike tells me. "I just gave her the heads-up."

"She won't believe we'll actually do it anyhow, but we have to," I say. "Maybe she'll get herself into treatment if she knows she is sectioned."

"Maureen, if being found dead at the bottom of the stairs isn't rock bottom, then what is?"

"Maybe rock bottom is a myth. Maybe with heroin, rock bottom is dead."

nine

Late Summer & Fall 2016

t is that time of the year: back-to-school time. Alongside families excitedly dropping their precious children off at college, cars filled to the brim with new sheets, microwaves, and mini-fridges to hold energy drinks to help those students stay awake while they cram for exams, I will drop Katie off like a litter of unwanted kittens, with her dirty clothes in one garbage bag.

Sectioning Katie and having the cops knocking on Bob the Scumbag's door at all hours of the day and night provide all the convincing Katie needs to take the scholarship that is offered at an incredible top-of-the-line, year-long program in Connecticut. She tries to dodge us for a while, but every time we get wind of where she is, Mike or I call the police. She bounces from one place to the next, then finally gives in and says she'll go. The program would have cost hundreds of thousands of dollars, but because it is just opening and needs a critical mass of patients, I am offered a scholarship for Katie, a free ride, for a year. It's the chance of a lifetime.

The phone rings nonstop all the way to Connecticut. I try not to answer unless Katie is sleeping, and that is most of the time. Mothers call for advice, people desperate for treatment call to see if I can help them get into detox. Facebook messages and texts pile up while I drive and drive and drive. It amazes me that while I can help others, I can't seem to help my own daughter, no matter how hard I try or how many connections I make.

After a couple of hours of driving, Katie starts to stir. There are fields of nothing on both sides of the highway as we pass the exit for Willington, Connecticut.

"Where the hell are we?"

"About halfway there," I say, waiting for her to freak out and laugh at the irony of *halfway*. Halfway to what, I wonder.

Instead she turns up the crappy music she knows I hate and starts bopping around in her seat. She opens up the bag of peanut M&Ms I bought her, and I glance over to see her texting on Facebook. Later I will read the blow-by-blow account of how high she is, how she is being forced into treatment one more time, and a video of me driving while she dances in her seat singing some obnoxious refrain from a rap song. The sadness in my face is so obvious that for weeks friends of hers will comment that she should be ashamed of herself for posting it. I only worry that it will upset her when she is better and looks at it again. I remind myself that this is not about me and wonder if it ever will be.

At least Liam will be off to UMass Amherst for his junior year of college, where he should have been all along. Coming home for his sophomore year had been a good decision; it was better for him to be home with me than alone in a dorm. He has been working and saving money for expenses beyond tuition. Getting him through four years of college without debt will be one of my proudest accomplishments. He has completely appreciated this by doing an exceptional job at school and working hard so he doesn't have to ask for anything during the year. I am so grateful that while I struggle with Katie, I also have had such pleasure in watching my son excel.

I park the car and glance down and realize Katie doesn't have shoes on.

"Where exactly are your shoes?"

She looks down at her feet like she just found them and says, "No idea."

"Brilliant! C'mon, let's hope you have shoes in one of these bags, and if not, I guess worse things have happened, right?"

I start walking, half-thinking she won't follow, searching for the correct address.

We step into the offices, set in a busy downtown area of New Haven, twenty minutes from the treatment center, and I am immediately taken in one direction and she in another. Everyone is young, beautiful, and polished. The place could pass for a modeling agency. The workers are clearly accustomed to dealing with a moneyed clientele, which I am not. There is actual art on the walls and real plants in ceramic pots.

I'm led into a glass-walled office and directed toward a buttery-soft leather chair that is nicer than anything I own. A perfectly groomed and stylishly dressed young man offers me a bottle of water from Sweden, which I take and chug, suddenly realizing how thirsty I am.

"Good afternoon," he says. "My name is Seth, and I'll be helping you through the admission process. I'm sure you want to see your daughter and where she will be living, but we find it's best if she goes directly from the offices with a staff member."

"Oh, Seth, Seth, Seth. I've been doing this for a long time, and I'm worn out. I'm holding on to the bottom of the chair right now for fear of creating a cartoonlike, body-shaped hole in the wall as I run the hell out of here. The miracle that I actually got her through the door is so huge that I'm more inclined to sneak out the back door before she changes her mind or have you tell me this is all a mistake."

Seth, who doesn't get this sort of response very often, bursts out laughing and walks around to close the door. He takes out the paperwork I need to sign and places it on the mahogany table he is using as a desk. My guess is that he is about thirty and maybe the oldest person in the office.

"You remind me of my mom," he says. "I came to the young men's program"—the new women's program is an offshoot of that one—"eight years ago on a scholarship. She fought for everything for me and she still won't tell me how she managed to get me in, but it was the best thing that ever happened to me. I've been sober ever since."

He can see the shock in my face, because there is no way to hide it.

He adds, "Everyone who works here is in recovery."

"You've got to be joking."

I glance backward, grateful for the glass walls, at the gorgeous, healthy-looking, busy members of the staff. For the first time, all day, I exhale.

As a parent, making that first step to seek out others who are like you might be the hardest you'll ever make. It's a meeting or an event, a 5K to raise awareness or a support group in an office building. *I don't belong here. I am not supposed to be here.* All that is an obstacle to overcome, and the sooner you know that, the sooner you can start learning. Luckily, there are more and more ways for people to break the silence.

Marion and I drive together to a vigil in Marlborough, Massachusetts, held on International Overdose Awareness Day, August 31. It's been four and half months since she lost Brian, and she has pushed herself to remain active at events and in fund-raising, having raised several thousand dollars in her son's name since his passing. She is strong, but I know that her calm demeanor is not always in step with her inner drumbeat.

We have honed our mission and developed a process of distributing funds. Watching the cycle of relapse, I've come to believe that the only effective way to combat it is to extend the continuum of care after detox and at least twenty-one additional days of treatment with sober, structured, recovery housing. This is where Magnolia can meet a need that isn't being met. People in recovery need to experience everything someone goes through in a year, the ups and downs, among other people who understand what they are feeling. Continuing to treat a relapsing brain disease as if it's a bout of flu is killing a whole generation.

We are early, but the crowd is building. On the front lawn of the Walker Building, 1,531 purple flags have been planted in the earth to signify the Massachusetts lives lost to overdose in the previous year. Marion and I both know the number will be higher next year, and we are acutely aware that in 2017, one of those flags will be for her son.

I see Kathy Leonard, who started this project in honor of her son; as always, she is quick to say hello. Warm and funny, she's always a welcome sight. You can hear the loss in her voice when she speaks of her son, as well as the fact that she is forever changed, but she continues to do all she can to make sense of his death by raising awareness. These flags will remain here for about two weeks, alerting anyone who drives by to the growing tragedy.

She hugs me and Marion and asks us what is going on with Magnolia. Kathy has heard how it is growing and has recently come to me for help for friends of her son's who need treatment.

"We are working with treatment centers that accept state insurance," I reply, "and arranging for four weeks of rent, approximately six hundred dollars, for people to go into sober living houses. The applicants write a letter stating what has happened to bring them to this point and why they believe they are ready to stay sober, and they are selected by the case managers and clinicians in the programs. The letters then go to Marion and Rhonda for approval."

"The letters are heartbreaking and amazing," Marion adds. "So many people wanting to get well and just can't seem to get it right."

Even with lots of help, raising tens of thousands of dollars without any paid staff, coupled with helping people find treatment, is more than a full-time job. I know I need to do something about my full-time insurance job becoming more of a hated hobby, but I am not sure how to keep all the plates in the air.

There's a large group of women and a few men, maybe seventy-five people, gathering on the hill in front of the flags to have their picture taken. They all carry pictures of their children. A few carry two pictures. There are photos of marines in uniforms, prom pictures, snapshots from dance recitals, and many, many graduation pictures. All of children lost to overdose. Many of them I know, but some are still unfamiliar.

Marion takes her place with her photo of Brian's smiling face.

"Is she okay?" asks another mom whose daughter is struggling.

"I guess she's about as okay as you could expect."

"I don't think she is grieving enough. I'm worried about her."

"I think everyone has their own way they grieve," I say, "and Marion is a helper, always has been. She is making a difference every day, and she does that in her son's name. I think that's how she deals with her heartache."

She nods at me, slightly put off, but I don't care. Recently, kind

Marion went to an event by herself. I was supposed to join her, but I couldn't make it. She left when someone remarked that they would never be going out so soon if their child had passed away.

"Son of a bitch!" I said when Marion told me this. "How the hell do they know what they would be doing if their child passed? That makes me so mad. What did you say?" I asked.

"I didn't say anything," she replied. "I just got my stuff and went in the car and cried all the way home."

"Fuck her, Marion! How dare she make you feel badly."

Marion laughed a little at how upset I'd gotten and told me not to worry. But I still do—I can't stand the idea of anyone hurting her. She's already had far more hurt than anyone deserves, especially her.

Two women head toward me. One seems heartbroken and is carrying a photo of a young man who looks exactly like her; the other, who stands taller, appears less broken. I see people now by their level of brokenness. The taller woman asks if it's okay if her sister has her picture taken with the group. The sister holds the picture up to me as if it is proof that she belongs.

"Of course, please go! Talk to someone afterward and join their group for support."

"It's a sad sight," the sister remarks as the mourning woman steps away, "so many grieving people. Barbara lost her son just a few weeks ago. You can see the sorrow and the pain in their faces," she adds.

Barbara comes back and thanks me. I explain to her about the Magnolia groups and quickly introduce her to Kathy, the event organizer, who is running around corralling the speakers and setting up the memorial slide show, adding more faces to the numbers of those lost. I call Marion over and explain to Barbara that she has also recently lost a son.

"Do you have other children?" Marion asks. "Brian was my only child."

"Yes, I have another son. His name is Kyle. I think he's finally ready to stop using heroin himself. I only wish I knew how to get him help. I can't lose another son."

Marion looks at me.

"Tell him to call me first thing in the morning. I'll help him. I promise." I hand Barbara my card and give her a hug, vowing silently to myself that if I can help it, she won't lose another son.

Most of the time when a mom is reaching out for her child, I never hear from them; but Kyle is different. He calls me first thing in the morning, and he is ready and willing to go to detox. He has just a hint of a southern accent, and I can sense that he hopes that I am telling him the truth though he doesn't fully believe I will help him. There is one snag. Although he has been living in Massachusetts, he has no way of proving it. All his identification is from Alabama. I need to get him signed up for MassHealth or a Department of Public Health bed, and that isn't going to be easy without identification.

The next day, the Friday before Labor Day weekend, after much finagling and a series of trains, buses, and some running to find a friend of mine before he leaves for the weekend, Kyle gets a bed in detox.

"Now, call me when you get there," I tell him, "and keep in touch while you're in detox. I can't help you if you don't call me."

"Yes, ma'am. I'll call you, I promise. I don't know why you're helping me, but I appreciate it."

"Just stick with it and call me so we can make a plan, Kyle. You need to have a plan."

A dichotomy of emotions—from the excitement of preparing Liam for college to the phone calls from the treatment center while another employee chases Katie down the street—has me constantly on the edge of my seat. I understand when people speak of feelings of PTSD from dealing with a child's addiction. I worry that I will never be the same. Every phone that rings or siren in the distance seems like bad news meant just for me. I find myself studying the expressions of people to decipher if there is something they aren't telling me. I am permanently rattled, waiting for the other shoe to drop, even when there are no shoes in sight.

Katie has talked of nothing but leaving. She lives in a mansion—plush, marbled, and luxurious—and is enrolled in a program designed around the needs of women under twenty-five. It is based on the treatment center's men's program, which has been incredibly successful for over twenty years, and she is miserable. She was the fourth person to walk through the doors and is receiving the sort of attention that only money can buy, and I expect she will be the first one out.

Like a rubber band, I'm stretched to the breaking point each time she tries to leave. Then she goes back and I try to return to normal, although I feel not quite the same with each decompression. Strained, I feel like I'm growing more and more brittle, having less and less give.

Liam and I are on the way to Whole Foods. My children have always liked going food shopping with me, and I enjoy having the time to talk to them. Today I'm on edge but trying to hold it together. The light turns red, and I glance down at my phone, which has just buzzed. It's a text from Chance, the administrator of the main Facebook support group, telling me about an incident in one of our groups. I look up just as the light turns green, but the woman behind me has already leaned on her horn. As I start to roll forward, she blasts the horn again, screaming and waving her arms, giving me the finger.

And that's when, without warning, I finally snap.

She passes me on the right, rolling down the window to shriek obscenities. I drive alongside her, screaming back, "Pull over, you bitch," forgetting that my son is sitting between us as I try to force her car off the road.

"Pull over because I'm going to kick your ass!" I yell at this woman in her little BMW, most likely going to Whole Foods as well, to shop for something green and organic. "C'mon, bitch, pull over."

She drives on the shoulder as I squeeze her off the road, and her expression changes to fear. She has met her crazy match. We both accelerate, and she gets ahead of me. I follow her, right on her bumper, but lose her when she makes a sharp left, blowing through a red light. I sit at the light, shaking, and look over at my son. He is horrified, and I am mortified.

"I can't believe I just acted like that."

"You can't believe it? Try watching it."

When the light changes, I turn and park in the Whole Foods lot, still trembling.

"I am so very sorry, Liam. I don't know what happened to me."

He says nothing, which is so much worse than anything he could have said. *It can't get any worse than this*, I tell myself. The phone rings, with a call from a Connecticut number.

Katie and another girl jumped over a wall of the facility, I'm told, and made an overly dramatic escape from a place where they could have easily walked out the front door. She left without her phone, clothes, or even shoes, with a girl who is from the area. The counselors estimate that she's been gone for about an hour.

Deflated from the psychotic break I just had, I am almost without a reaction. Later I'll find out—off the record, due to HIPAA— that she ended up overdosing that evening and landed in a Connecticut hospital. Then she called Bob the Scumbag, and he picked her up yet again. She has lasted less than a month.

Bob the Scumbag texts me to tell me how bad a situation Katie is in. He explains in detail how many times he has administered Narcan to her, leaving out that he was, in fact, the person who took her to purchase the drugs and most likely bought them for her. He wants me to be grateful because he believes no one else she knows would keep Narcan on hand for her. He boasts, speaking like a medical professional, that the last time he revived her it required "4 of 4ml = 16 ml of Narcan" and CPR, which, luckily, he was there to administer. He addresses me as "Dear Maureen," which makes bile rise in my throat.

Life goes on, and the phone continues to ring day and night. The calls are different but more or less the same until the one from the FBI. It's not every day that happens. The agents are looking for Susanna and are calling me because they heard I helped get her into treatment. The thought of the FBI having heard about anything I did gives me the creeps.

Special Agent Dow from the Boston Task Force on Human Trafficking wants to get in touch with Susanna because she is one of the more important witnesses in the Kilby Street Gang case.

"Do you know where she is?" Agent Dow asks.

My first inclination is to lie. I don't know why, but I feel like I should protect Susanna from the FBI.

The agent must sense my uneasiness, because she adds, "She's actually in danger if these people get back on the streets."

Susanna had relapsed and called to tell me she had an abscess from shooting into her leg and was really sick. I had finally convinced her to go to the emergency department at Brockton Hospital, but she left when they wanted to admit her. Recently she had just gone back, worse than before. I was hoping she'd let me get her back into detox, which she was fighting. I was sure she'd leave the ED the minute she started to withdraw.

"I'll make a deal with you," I tell Agent Dow. "I'll tell you where she is if you help me section her. I'm afraid she's going to die or lose her leg. She's sick, and she needs detox."

"You have a deal," Agent Dow responds.

Several hours later, the phone rings. It is Susanna, furious. "You sectioned me! You sectioned me? How could you do that? I need to want this. You can't just do that to someone. I'm never speaking to you ever again."

"You can do that if you want, but I'll take every opportunity I can to save your life until you want to save it, too. I care about you, Susanna, and I hope you change your mind about talking to me. I'd miss you if you didn't."

I'm not sure if she hears what I say because she is no longer on the line.

It's hot and humid as I walk out of the conference in Hyannis and get in my car. The Cape Cod Symposium on Addictive Disorders is one of the most well-attended addiction conferences, and I've just spent days listening to one speaker after another. I'm fortunate to be able to go to the condo in Brewster instead of having to take a room in the convention hotel, which is not getting good reviews from the people staying there. I start my car and look at Facebook for the first time all day. Everywhere a video is being shared. I glance at it briefly and can't believe my eyes. A woman has overdosed, and her child is trying to shake her awake. They seem to be in the aisle of a store, and I can see that someone is standing next to the person filming.

Why am I seeing this? Who would film something like this, and why is anyone sharing this? I am horrified and furious. I won't look at it anymore. I stop the video.

What is happening? We're trying to change this and finally making progress! I've become part of Facing Addiction and a subgroup that is attempting to end the stigma of addiction by changing the language. We are carefully referring to *people with a substance use disorder* instead of saying *addicts* or, even worse, *junkies*; we talk about *testing positive* or *negative* instead of *clean* or *dirty*. We are seeing change. But things like this video hinder our progress.

On September 22, 2016, the video goes viral. It is everywhere. Television news channels replay the segment over and over. The CBS local affiliate and every other news station in the area reports on this woman, giving her a reality-TV-star status she loathes. I refuse to watch it. I know what it's like to have the media make a horrific situation worse. I won't be a part of it, and I can't be silent.

A typical report is the one from the *Washington Post* that opens:

A terrified toddler in pink-and-purple "Frozen" pajamas prodded, pulled and cried—but was powerless to wake up her mother.

Mandy McGowan, 36, was unconscious from an apparent opioid overdose, sprawled in the toy aisle of a Family Dollar store in Lawrence, Mass. Her 2-year-old daughter pulled McGowan's fingers, then sat down beside her and tried to shake her face.

The heart-wrenching moment was captured on video, and the footage went viral—another shocking scene from the opioid epidemic's harrowing horror show.

I remove the link from the Facebook pages, as well as any reference to the stigmatizing video. I will not tolerate someone who could have been any one of our children being crucified in that way. Although I know it's nothing new; once again, Nathaniel Hawthorne had already diagnosed the problem long ago:

> But there is a fatality, a feeling so irresistible and inevitable that it
> has the force of doom, which almost invariably compels human
> beings to linger around and haunt, ghostlike, the spot where some
> great and marked event has given the color to their lifetime. . . .
> The chain that bound her here was of iron links, and galling to
> her inmost soul, but could never be broken.

A Magnolia member calls to say that Mandy is about to be evicted from her home in New Hampshire; she is dope-sick and desperate. Friends are afraid she will try to kill herself. Her daughter, who was taken into protective custody, was her world.

"Can I put you in touch with her? She wants help."

"Yes! Yes! Please do!"

Mandy is a New Hampshire resident, but there is nothing for her in New Hampshire. All the clinics are full, with days or, more likely, weeks of waiting before Mandy can get in, and with the notoriety, no one even wants to discuss helping her. She isn't a Massachusetts resident and, therefore, is not eligible for detox through MassHealth. I call everyone I can think of who might be able to pull some strings, but come up empty. Everyone knows her name and her face.

After the overdose, she had been brought to a hospital just over the border in Methuen, but she was released the next day when hospital personnel realized who she was and that she was not, in fact, a resident of Massachusetts. She was withdrawing and suffering and no one cared—yet they expected her not to continue to use. She wants her daughter back, and that is all she says when I speak to her. "I'll do my best to help you," I promise.

Earlier that year, Matt Ganem had opened a Banyan Treatment Center in Wilmington, Massachusetts. It was his dream to run his own facility, and I am so proud of how far he has come. He is a constant source of support and information, and he deserves every good thing life has to offer.

"Matt, I have a problem."

"Okay, let's hear it."

"Have you seen the video of the woman who overdosed with her child in the dollar store?"

"Don't even get me started about that fucking video."

"I know, I know. Well, she needs help, and she contacted me. No insurance. New Hampshire resident. They took her kid and told her if she ever wanted to see her, she needed to get into treatment, but the courts offered nothing and no one will take her. She has pretty much detoxed on her own and is sitting in an empty house with no electricity, waiting to be evicted or kill herself. It's a coin toss at this point."

"Bring her in."

"Thank you, Matthew. When are you going to let me adopt you?"

"Soon, Mama, soon." He laughs.

I give him her contact information.

"I'll call you with the ETA."

What the fuck is wrong with people? I think. This surpasses my anger at *Saturday Night Live*. What has the world turned into? The carelessness and the inhumanity of three separate people filming someone overdosing, and doing so without offering to help her child, makes me livid. I am angry for Mandy, but I am also angry for Katie. I can't stand by while any suffering human being is exploited in this way. I navigate back to Facebook and post Martin Niemöller's poem "First They Came," because it is about the importance of speaking out:

> First they came for the Communists, and I did not
>   speak out—
> because I was not a Communist;
> Then they came for the socialists, and I did not
>   speak out—
> because I was not a socialist;
> Then they came for the trade unionists, and I did
>   not speak out—
> because I was not a trade unionist;
> Then they came for the Jews, and I did not speak
>   out—
> because I was not a Jew;
> Then they came for me—
> and there was no one left to speak for me.

This is not okay, and I need to keep reminding people that stigma is what kills people. Silence is death. Hiding a disease is what created this situation. Now, though, several media outlets contact people who know Mandy in New Hampshire, and at least one of them discloses who got her into treatment. I am inundated with calls. *NBC Nightly News with Lester Holt*, *The Doctors*, Dr. Oz, MTV, and every print or broadcast organization large and small seems to have my number or e-mail address. I do not speak to any of them, and I refuse to divulge Mandy's whereabouts, although I pass the information along to Matt.

Finally, Katharine Seelye, New England bureau chief for the *New York Times*, calls. She is writing an article and wants to know if I will comment. She plans on mentioning Magnolia and noting that I found Mandy the bed in treatment, as others have reported, and she wants to know what I think about the video.

I connect with Kit. She's smart, compassionate, and concerned about doing the story justice. I trust her and give her my thoughts.

The attention causes Magnolia's Facebook groups to explode to over ten thousand members across the United States and in Canada before the end of the October. Donations from around the country follow. We can help more people because of the publicity. The media's focus becomes a blessing and a curse.

Around the same time, Katie, now knowing as much as I do about getting into treatment, calls a center in Haverhill, Serenity at Summit, and arranges for her own detox. The evening before she goes in, she sits down with Kit Seelye and tells her story.

Katie reveals herself to Kit and the photographer as she waits, sick and in withdrawal, to leave for detox. She sits in the window catching the last of the day's light. She's still beautiful, but her eyes are dull and sad. She steps outside on the front porch, and the photographer takes a few more shots. Her oversized sweater rides up her arm slightly, revealing her tattoo that says "freedom," with small birds flying off the "m." They ask her to pull the sleeve up a bit more and a long, angry track mark is revealed.

It takes months before the article comes out, but when it does, it's no surprise to see that the editors have chosen that photo for the cover.

The article ends with a quote from me, reflecting the way I end all my conversations with parents, the only true thing I know for sure:

"Tell your children you love them, because 'it might be the last thing you say to them.'"

ten | Winter 2017

"Hey, sweetie, how are you?"

"I'm good, Mommy. I'm going to a sober event with the rest of the people at the treatment center for New Year's Eve. So, I'm trying to figure out what to wear."

"Well, that sounds pretty normal considering, huh?"

The reality is that Katie has been in some form of treatment for the holidays for the last three years, and this year is no exception. Each year we hope that next year will be different. We know that it could be worse, but the truth is that it's been a very long time since she was home and either not high or counting the moments until she can leave and get high.

"Yeah, I guess so—better than last year. Hey, can I ask you for a favor? It's kind of big."

"No money, Katie. I can't do it," I respond, anticipating that she'll ask for either money or clothes. She has lost every type of article of clothing several times over, and I'm sick of replacing things for her.

Along with that, she's "borrowed" a lot of my clothes, items I'll never see again.

"No, Mom, it's not for me—well, not directly. Can you help Gabe Wright? I told him you would, but he thinks you hate him."

Gabe Wright, the person who we've blamed for getting Katie addicted to heroin, the person who first showed her how to use a needle.

"Mom?"

I take a deep breath, then another. If I believe, as I say I do, that this is a disease, that I cannot hold against Katie the things she has done when she was consumed by addiction, that every person deserves treatment, then I should help him. I need to put my money where my mouth is.

"Of course, I'll help him, Katie. Tell him to call me."

I grab my old boyfriends Ben and Jerry out of the fridge and make a late lunch of a pint of Peanut Butter Cup while I wait for the call. When I pull up the open detox bed list on my phone, as I expected, there is nothing.

It's two o'clock on Friday, December 30, and I'm just about to leave for the Cape. Randy is waiting for me down there, and we have plans. How the hell am I going to find Gabe help?

Digging deep into my mental list of contacts, I call a treatment center that does a great job with its MassHealth patients. The counselors there are understaffed, overworked, and underpaid, but they have an abundance of compassion. No fancy buildings or massage therapists but a staff that cares; plus, I've got a friend in admissions. I've made this contact because Magnolia helps the facility with sober living scholarships for some of its patients who complete the longer-term programs. I call Judy on her cell, and she answers right away.

"Hello, my friend," I say. "Happy New Year!"

"Oh, Lord, let's hope so," Judy answers. "How are you?"

"I'm good, but I have a friend who isn't doing so well. Twenty-six-year-old male, needs detox, heroin, MassHealth. Tell me you have a bed?"

"How can I say no to you? How soon can you have him here?"

"I'm going to pick him up as soon as he calls me, and I should be on the road in about fifteen minutes. It will take me about two hours to get to you."

"Perfect! I'll wait for you. It will be good to see you."

An unfamiliar number appears on my caller ID. I answer on the first ring, so I don't have to think about whether I want to let it go to voice mail.

"Hi, Maureen. I'm Katie's friend Gabe. She said you could help me."

"Gabriel Wright. Where are you now?"

There's traffic in the background as he answers: "I'm in Salem."

"There are a few conditions, Gabe. You have to finish detox and then go on to a longer-term program. I am not helping you get sober if you're planning on leaving right after detox. That's just setting you up to overdose, and I'm not doing that. In order to make that happen, you have to put me on your release and call me, because if you don't call me while you're in detox, I can't help you. You also have to pack your stuff up right now and be ready to go. Can you do that?"

There is quiet on the other end of the line, and I mistake it for disagreement when, in fact, it is disbelief that I am going to help him.

"Everything I own is in my duffel bag on my back. I've been homeless for three months. If you help me, I'll do whatever you tell me to do, but if you could give me twenty minutes I'd appreciate it."

I can hear the pain and desperation in his voice. He is nothing like I expected. I want to cry, not only for him but for all the misconceptions that I, and others, have about those who suffer with this disease. I picture his father at the back of the room in the Learn to Cope meetings and imagine Gabe as a child playing baseball, bringing home his spelling test, doing a cannonball into a pool.

"Okay, hon," I say, "it's going to be okay. I have a bed for you tonight. It's a good place but it's a couple of hours away, so we have to move quickly. I'm leaving in a few minutes. Tell me exactly where you are, and I'll be right there."

I call Judy back and say that I'm on my way and that he will be calling shortly. She can tell something is wrong.

"What's up?" she asks.

"Oh, it's the kid my daughter first started shooting up with. I've spent a long time blaming him, and I just heard the voice of every kid who is suffering on the other end of the phone. We're on our way. He'll do the intake from the car."

I'm about to cry and I don't have time for that, so I rush Judy off the phone.

The light is fading and I'm going to get stuck in traffic on the way down—that I know. I throw my bag in the car and make my way into Salem. Ten minutes remain before I am to meet Gabe. Wasting time, I drive past 250 Washington and turn onto Derby Street. As I swing past the Salem Common, I glance up at the statue of Nathaniel Hawthorne.

I wonder, will Katie be forever branded? Will there ever be a time when she can look at herself as anything other than the collateral damage of the last few years?

There is an older man standing where Gabe told me to meet him, but no Gabe. I check the clock in my car, aware that if I don't get on the road soon, it's going to take an extra hour to get there. The guy standing where Gabe should be looks over and starts to walk toward me. I'm readying myself to tell him I don't have any change when he grabs a duffel bag and I realize it's Gabe. A stranger gets into my car, dirty, hat pulled down over blond hair so dirty it looks brown; his face is sunken in due to loss of weight or teeth—most likely both.

"Thank you so much, I really appreciate this," he says as he throws his duffel bag in the back seat and jumps into the front.

It takes me a moment to register that this old man is actually twenty-six years old. I'm reminded of the story of Charlie Parker; the coroner deduced from examining the corpse that the man was sixty years old, judging by the condition of his liver and heart and other organs. Parker was only thirty-four. The disease is taking them younger and younger now, not giving them a chance to make a mark.

"Do you want to stop for coffee or something to eat before we get on the road?"

"No, I'm good. My dad gave me a Dunkin' Donuts gift card for Christmas, so I just ate there."

Gabe does the intake, and we drive in silence for a while. Then he confesses to me how many times he fixed the car when Katie was using it. She is a worse driver than I had even known; he repaired the mirrors she had ripped off and the smaller dents I never knew about. He also called the police when she overdosed and stayed with her and gave her CPR. I had no idea. He is sad, broken, and just high enough not to be too sick. He dozes off for the last ninety minutes of the drive. I have to remind him to call his parents before he goes in.

Thank God I am warned that the *New York Times* article will come out this Sunday, January 8, because when I open the paper, the sight of my daughter's track-marked wrist, with "freedom" written across it and under the scars, takes my breath away. Just that photo of her wrist shakes me. It tells the story of her desperation to be free of the scars: not only of the heroin but of the trauma and the disease that creates the addiction. I stare at the photograph, unable to move on from it to read the article.

I think of Gabe Wright and wonder how he is. He's shut down, and I can rarely get more than a few words out of him when he does call. He has just a couple of weeks left, and he will then be transferred to a longer-term program. Once he gets some time behind him in that program, he will move on to sober living.

He is so depressed, and I worry that he will give up and leave. So, after he begins the ninety-day program, I drive the almost two hours to visit him.

The facility is new and resembles a college more than a hospital. People are in varying stages of recovery and run the gamut from those who look like they are sick and broken to those who leave you guessing if they are patient or employee. We meet in the Family Room, which is completely glass-enclosed. He has gained weight, his face is clear, and he seems healthy. His hair is long and blond and curls slightly around his face. His eyes are a brilliant blue, and they sparkle. He's gained no less than thirty well-needed pounds. He's cute and barely looks his age. It's almost a miracle, and the shock is written all over my face.

"Oh, my God, you're frigging adorable," I say, smacking him in the arm.

"Of course I am." He laughs.

I've never heard him laugh before, and it warms my heart.

We make some small talk. He's doing well. He's funny and optimistic and looking forward to the future. He covers his mouth when he talks or laughs. The loss of teeth and awful dental problems are the norm for people addicted to drugs. I decide to be straight with him.

"You are too young and cute not to have teeth. What are we going to do about it?"

"I'm not sure. I had an upper plate, but I lost it when I was fucked up, and MassHealth only pays for one every seven years. That gives me five more years of this. They won't take me for outside appointments here, anyway."

"Yeah, that's not happening. You can't go out into the world, as cute as you are, and start over without teeth at your age. I'll take you. You figure out the least expensive place to go as close as possible to this facility, and I'll take you. They'll let me take you out for that."

"Are you sure?"

"You've got to learn to trust me, Gabriel. I always do what I say I'm going to do. Now, call me more going forward. I can't help you if you don't call me."

Katie's life over the last six months has been a continuous stream of entering and exiting facilities. It has taken a toll on everyone. I try to behave like a normal mother, girlfriend, business owner, but I'm walking a high ledge, knowing that any moment I could plummet to the ground.

I'm tired of being me, of being around myself, and I know that something needs to change. I've been holding everything in as best I can because I don't want anything else to fall apart. Yet recently I have begun to relax, finally. Katie has gone, willingly, to a very strong twelve-step program at a place called the Plymouth House. It cost more than four thousand dollars, so even with her dad's help, I'll be paying it off for a while.

Randy and I are eating dinner together, then heading to the Cape, and once we get there, it will all be better. I just have to make it to the Cape. Increasingly, the Cape is where I see myself when I dream.

Not sleeping dreams—at least I don't think so—but those daydreams that are more real because you're awake only so tired you shouldn't be. When I go to a happy place in those dreams, I go to the Cape. There the ocean folds and unfolds, endlessly, and the horizon recedes. There is a great sense of possibility out there where the sky sinks into the ocean.

The phone rings, and it's a call from New Hampshire. I answer thinking it's Katie but hear the voice of the director. Katie has decided to leave. I hang up.

"You should go home," Randy says. "If she comes to your house, Liam is there alone and they might need you."

"I don't want to, though. I want to go with you, to the Cape. What about me? What about what I need?"

"Come in the morning."

I know he doesn't want me to come in the morning. He is as tired of this as I am. He can walk away. I know that. He didn't sign up for this. I feel another thing I love slipping through my fingers.

I want to run away. It's too much, not just for Katie but for me, and for everyone who loves either of us. The only thing that keeps me from following through on my wished-for escape is the promise I made to Katie months ago.

She was sitting on the floor of my kitchen at three a.m., just dropped off by some good sober friends who had been searching for her all night following a relapse. It was a shock, once again, because she had been doing so well. I was awoken by banging on my bedroom window, and it took a few heart-pounding moments before I realized that people coming to murder you rarely knock on the window and that it was, in fact, Katie. Half-asleep, hair sticking straight up, blind without my glasses, and in my ratty "I sleep alone" pajamas, I convinced Katie and company to go to the front door, where she tried to bolt again, realizing that everyone was going home rather than coming in with her. Three people tried to keep her from running until, with a burst of adrenaline and looking like a lunatic I'm sure, I picked her up by both shoulders and threw her into the house, slamming the door and ending the conversation over whether to stay or go.

I could see she was covered with vomit as she ran into the kitchen to get a knife from the drawer, first threatening to stab herself, then waving it at me. I reached out and smacked her across the face, something I had never done in her twenty-four years on this earth. I cannot begin to express how much I needed to slap her. In fact, I have never wanted to slap anyone so much in my life.

She crumbled to the floor crying that she wanted to die.

"Why won't you let me go?" she begged. "If you love me you'd let me die."

I thought about it in that moment: *How selfish am I? This poor child is in such incredible pain. Am I fighting harder than she is for my own reasons and my fear of losing her? How much does she have to suffer before I do let go?*

Those thoughts passed quickly and I picked her up off the floor, full of vomit and snot, her pupils completely pinlike and her eyes glassy, and asked her an important question: if she wanted to wear my penguin pajamas. She cried harder, saying yes, and changed in the middle of the kitchen, then crawled into bed with me, covered in pink skiing penguins, and fell asleep with her head on my chest. I listened to her breathing and watched her eyelashes flutter as she slept, and it broke my heart, which I sincerely thought couldn't break anymore.

"There is no letting go, Ladybug," I whispered to her. "Never going to happen."

And that pledge, not to let go, is how I find myself in my car in the middle of March with a baseball bat on the passenger seat next to me, on my way to kill Bob the Scumbag. The phone is ringing, and I pick it up and decide to answer.

"Have you heard anything?" Mike asks.

"Yeah, they called me to tell me she was packing about three hours ago. They told me not to come over. They said they were going to call the police if she left and let them pick her up, but I have a bad feeling."

"What do you mean, a bad feeling?"

"I just think that fucker is going to pick her up and keep using her up and then she's going to die."

"Jesus, don't say that! What do we do?"

"I've decided to kill him. I have Liam's bat, and when I see him, I'm going to beat his head in so that he can't ever do this to anyone else."

We have recently found out that Bob the Scumbag's surname is not actually "the Scumbag," allowing us to Google him and learn that some of the things he has done to Katie—buying her drugs, cutting her off from treatment, hiding her from the police—are things he had done before. We uncovered another story, this one about a young woman who was married with small children when he became involved with her. His sick, perverted need to see her die and then revive her resulted in the young woman's husband, who had no criminal record, stabbing Bob nearly to death. Even after spending two years in jail, the husband said that his only regret was not killing Bob. He promised that he will try it again if he has to.

Mike breaks the silence and tells me not to let anyone see me.

"You can say it was self-defense. Just don't let anyone see you."

"Remember how happy we were when all of the prenatal tests came back and we found out that she was a healthy little girl? Did you ever think we would be here?"

"No, never once did any of this cross my mind."

I hang up the phone and turn off the ringer and the radio.

I pull into the parking lot of the treatment center and make a circle around the parked cars, looking into each one. No one. I go around the back of the building, into the parking lots of the nearby buildings, then make another slow crawl past the Center's massive glass front door. When I see a car pull into the lot, I reach over and touch the top of the bat. The car parks and is still for a moment. The door opens, and a short black woman in nurse's scrubs gets out. I let go of the bat.

I know that the counselors here are good at convincing people to stay, and they did promise to call me if Katie was still intent on leaving. Maybe my feeling is wrong. I've cruised around the lot one more time and am swinging past the front door when she spots me through it and I her. Her pace quickens as she nears the door, dragging a giant brown suitcase we used when we went to Disney World. She opens the front door and tries to throw it at my car. She runs back in, screaming at everyone, most likely thinking they tipped me off, grabs two paper bags of her things and throws those a little more easily at the car. I catch her glancing across the parking lot and see a red truck and a man who could only be Bob. Taking a deep breath, I am tempted to put the car in drive and do what I came to do. Instead, I pretend like I haven't seen him and try to talk to Katie.

"What are you doing here?" she yells. "I canceled the release. I told them not to tell you. That's wrong. Why did they do that? You can't make me go with you, and I'm not going back in there!"

A wave of calm floods over me, and I modulate my voice: "No

one told me, Katie. You know how connected we are. I just had a feeling that I needed to come, so I did."

"What do you want?"

I stick my arm out of the car, extending my hand toward her. I can see employees I know gathered in the big glass-walled waiting area. I shake my head no so that they won't come out.

"Just talk to me for a second, sweetie. Hold my hand."

I extend my body as far as I can, and she takes my hand.

"Mom, please just let me go. I've had enough."

"I can't, sweetie. You're freezing, baby—just get in the car for a second and we can talk."

"No, you're going to take off with me."

"Well, I can understand why you would say that, but look—" I take the keys out of the ignition and drop them on the floor of the car. "No keys, so I'm not going anywhere."

She climbs into the passenger side of the RAV4 and quickly makes eye contact with Bob on the other side of the lot. She moves the bat over as she closes the door. "Why is Liam's bat in the car?"

"I'm going to kill Bob with it."

"What did you just say?"

"I'm going to beat Bob until he is dead with this bat."

"You can't keep me from getting high, even if you kill Bob."

"I realize that, Katie, but I can keep Bob from destroying anyone else. I can keep him from hurting you any more, from picking you up, from convincing you to leave treatment, and I can keep him from infecting this world with his presence. I can't keep you from heroin, and you can't keep me from doing what I need to do."

"Jesus, Mom."

"What are you planning on doing when you leave and get high? Do you think life will get better? That it will be different than it was before? If you go back to that disgusting piece of shit again, I just don't know what I'll do," I tell Katie.

"He is the fucking devil himself, don't you see that? You know that one of these times when you overdose with him watching you it will be the last, and then he will toss your body off the side of the highway because he's not going to want to get involved. Is that what you want? You want me identifying your body after it's been in the woods for a week or two?"

She shakes her head no, but says nothing. I've never talked to her like this before. Some limit has been surpassed, and yet I press on.

"Listen to me, little girl: I couldn't love you any more than I do, but I need to start loving myself just as much. I cannot do this anymore. It doesn't mean I don't love you or that I won't help you when you are serious about getting help. It also doesn't mean that I won't section you and make sure you are put somewhere safe if I think I can. What it does mean is that from this moment, I am going to start to put as much energy as I've put into saving your life into saving mine. This is killing me and your father, and I don't want to go down with you. Do understand that? This is literally killing us and you at the same time."

She leans over and puts her head on her knees and sobs.

"I'm sorry, Mom. I have to stop. I don't want to do this to you and Dad and Liam anymore."

"Put your seat belt on. I'll drive you back to treatment at Serenity tomorrow morning. This time needs to be different."

eleven | Spring 2017

S ubstance use disorder is like being denied the right to vote: it's very hard for most people to imagine or care about it unless it affects them personally. Why should we be concerned about a minority of people who can't seem to exercise self-control? The false and harmful perception that substance use disorder is a moral failing runs deep, going all the way back to Hawthorne, or the Hathornes, back to the first thin-lipped Pilgrims who came ashore to make a city upon a hill. It is always easier to say *this can't happen to me* than to admit or worry that you might be next. The shock is very great when it does happen, and the saddest thing I hear so many young people say is "I didn't come from this." I hear it again and again: "I didn't come from this." Their hands are up in disbelief, they are referring to their clothes, their teeth (or lack of them), or their surroundings (no sheets, possessions in garbage bags). "I didn't come from this." They mean they have family who love them, or used to, and they had houses they grew up in. Most young people don't come from "this." I understand their total shell shock, but I also know what "this" is. I came from it.

I grew up in a high-ranch-style house on a dead-end street lined with trees in Lake Ronkonkoma, New York. The town was notable only for an Indian legend of a haunted lake that was rumored to drown a young man each summer. My mother swore that the entire town was built on an Indian burial ground and, therefore, cursed.

In this small town, most of the residents were the first generation to leave the city behind: on the holidays, we all went to Brooklyn or Queens to visit grandparents. It was the 1960s, and young families with 2.5 children picked a location on Long Island in direct relation to what they could afford to pay for a house. Nassau County was for professionals, Suffolk for the trades. Most everyone had a dog, the schools were good, vacations were done in tents, carnivals were held in each town by the fire department, and everyone had brothers and sisters. I lived the exception.

My house was a sad, dark place soaked in alcohol, ready to leap into flames. I was a solitary sort of child. In the late afternoon when the shadows grew long and my mother would pick up the bottle, I would ride my bike up the hill at the corner of University Drive and Portion Road and coast down as fast as I could, pretending to fly far away. That feeling of freedom was intoxicating, and I would turn around at the end of the cul-de-sac and do it over and over until the lights came on and I had to go back into the house.

The first drink of the day started earlier and earlier, until by my teenage years there was little to differentiate between day and night. My father would join her the minute he got home from work, and it was all good between them until one of them took the drink that knocked down the house of cards. As a kindergartener, I'd set a manually winding Timex alarm clock that glowed green numbers in the dark for six-thirty in the morning. Waking and getting dressed, feeding myself a completely inappropriate breakfast of Yankee Doodles cupcakes and Carnation Instant Breakfast, readying myself for school and getting to the bus on time, quietly and in the dark, so as not to bother anyone each morning.

At the age of ten, I was once woken up while a party raged in another room, then shoved into the bathroom, where I was expected to clean up my mother. She was covered with vomit and had shit all over herself and the bathroom floor.

"Be quiet," my father whispered. "Don't let anyone know." He locked the door behind himself as he left.

I didn't need either directive. There was the weekly embarrassment of the local liquor store delivering cases of beer and liquor at the same time each Friday, ironically just as the yellow school bus made the turn in the cul-de-sac in front of my house. Being woken in the middle of the night by my father beating my drunken mother; running to jump on his back to make him stop; her face turning blue in the grip of his hands around her throat; the familiar sight of the police taking him away.

These are my childhood memories. My mother's wedding rings, along with a suicide note, were routinely found in the morning on my dresser, or I'd come upon her drunk and passed out somewhere in the house, outside the house, or at a much-dreaded family event— and all of these things were met with my father telling me, "Do you know how much she loves you? You should be able to see that."

I learned to distrust my own understanding of a situation. I learned to believe my mother was right: the myth of the Indian burial was true, the town was cursed—or at least I was.

Finally, I got angry and fought back. As far as I could see, my parents were just getting in the way of me finishing school and leaving that hellhole they insisted I was lucky to have. In that quiet, middle-to-lower-middle-class suburban neighborhood, everyone knew that something was "off" and had been for many years, yet no one did anything to help. People minded their own business. I spoke to my guidance counselor privately and was blessed to find a compassionate ear. I didn't just want someone to listen; I wanted answers. I probed and planned and eventually packed a bag and, on the counselor's instruction, walked a familiar route to the corner 7-Eleven pay phone to call Seabury Barn, a local shelter for homeless and runaway teens.

Seabury Barn was the land of the misfit toys. In a time when people did not just lose custody of their children, this large, old ramshackle house set on a hill in Stony Brook, an otherwise well-to-do area of Long Island, was chock-full of young teenagers who had been abused, neglected, or otherwise thrown away. With boys on one floor, girls on another, we had limited oversight and rarely left the house. Spending the first three months of tenth grade there, planning my next move, I found a way each week to get my homework and tests delivered and picked up and kept up with my schoolwork. My parents lost custody of me to the state when I was declared an emancipated minor at sixteen. I was free.

I don't like to talk about this part of my past, and my therapist, Candace, understands this by now, after ten years. Instead, I like to tell her the good news in my life.

I tell her that Mandy McGowan has been free of drugs for a year and regularly travels all the way to New Hampshire to see her daughter, despite still being harassed by Internet trolls. I tell her about the news from the Associated Press. In its stylebook, the bible for journalists, the AP released new guidelines recommending that reporters "avoid words like *alcoholic, addict, user* and *abuser* unless they are in quotations or names of organizations"—such as the National Institute on Drug Abuse or Alcoholics Anonymous—and, "instead, choose phrasing like *he was addicted, people with heroin addiction*, or *he used drugs*." It is a subtle change, but it's what we're fighting for. I tell Candace about Gabe Wright, how I helped him get a new set of teeth and a sober place to live. The last time I called him, he didn't pick up. He was in church. I had told Gabe Wright what I tell everyone: "It's not enough to not want to get high; you have to want to be sober. It's work to be alive. You need to be ready to do the work." He seems to be.

Candace stops me.

"What's going on with you?"

I used to dread that question. "What *isn't* going on with me?" I would've joked. But I know by the tone of Candace's voice and my general understanding of psychology that she means, "Maureen, you've said a lot about how other people are doing. But what about you?"

It's the first time in a long time that I am happy to answer that question.

"I'm good. Randy and I had a rough time of it, but we are doing better now. Believe it or not, I turn off my phone at night and when we're together on the weekend."

"The whole weekend?"

"It's made all the difference. I had to take my life back. None of what I was doing was good for me, and it wasn't helping Katie. She has gotten to the point where she can get herself into treatment. I've introduced her to so many people to reach out to if she wants, and she knows what to do to find help. I had to save myself. As for Katie, it's been brutal. She's been in treatment more than she's been out. But, at the moment, so far as I know, she is safe. She knows I love her; I tell her every day."

———

wonder what ever happened to Olivia Rose, the girl whose mom was
dropping off clothes in detox? What ever happened to all the people
whose lives and journeys I've glimpsed a fragment of? It's not unusual
now for me to help thirty or more people per month into some
form of treatment. Some of them stay in touch or come back for help
with getting into treatment again. Sometimes I've gotten to know
their parents and they join the Magnolia groups, so I hear how the
children are doing. So many others just disappear, and some of them
haunt me. I try not to get too emotionally involved, but it's almost
impossible.

Another late-summer day, and I'm listening to a young girl give
me reasons why she can't go to treatment and looking for signs that
she is willing.

"I have been to every detox in Massachusetts," says Nikki. "I have
a warrant for a probation violation because I just can't stay clean.
Maybe I should just go to jail and do some time and get it over with."

"That's an option. Do you want to go to jail?"

The reality of that choice brings her to tears. We are sitting in the
park in Salem across from 250 Washington Street. I spot a needle in
the grass across the sidewalk and remind myself to call the police
department to collect it and the others that are doubtless scattered
around.

To be willing to truly benefit from treatment, you need to know
that you're helpless against the disease—and then right away, when
you're in recovery, you need a support system that will tell you that
you're not hopeless. That's the trick. Then you have to believe it—
and find a way to keep putting yourself into situations where that is
reinforced. If it sounds difficult, it's because it is very difficult.

"Let me just call and see if there's a bed," I tell Nikki. "Then we
can keep talking."

I dial Sammy, the first person I ever helped get into treatment, years ago now. Sammy is a dynamo. She works at one of the better MassHealth treatment centers, in Brockton, and as a recovery coach at a nearby hospital.

"Hey, sweetie, it's Maureen. I'm sitting with a friend, and she needs a bed. Do you know if you have any discharges?"

She does, so I give her Nikki's name and date of birth.

"Okay," I say to Nikki, "you can call this number and do the intake and make some changes, or we can sit here and talk and everything stays exactly as it is. It's your choice."

My phone rings; it's Katie. Nikki is bent over, crying, with her head resting in her hands. I rub her back with my free hand. An older woman walking a dog while holding the hand of a toddler glances at us, then moves to the other side of the path. The child begins to slow near the needle, and I warn the woman, who grabs his hand and pulls him away, shaking her head. She thinks it is my needle and that we are both high.

"Mom, it was thirteen overdoses. We forgot the one at the bottom of the stairs."

She is in treatment again. And we'd spoken yesterday, as she was doing intake, about how many times she'd overdosed. It's not so much that you get used to the idea of your child floating between life and death that many times; it's more that a numbness sets in that can only be a survival instinct. The week before Katie went in, she OD'd three times in less than four days, during the last one needing CPR and four doses of Narcan. She promises that it is the last one. I worry that it will be, but not for any reason I can bear thinking about.

"Did you get my letter?" she asks.

"I did. Thank you. I love your letters. I'll put it in the drawer with the rest of them."

The drawer that once held my jewelry now holds her letters and cards, as a reminder that while some objects are missing, I still have my daughter, and that is full of possibilities. I've been carrying this one around with me, and I reach into my purse and touch it as I listen to Nikki wipe away some of her snot and tears. I've read it so many times, I have it nearly memorized.

Hey Mom,
I woke up wanting to write you a letter. I remembered how I use [sic] to do it all the time. I guess it just got old after all the programs and broken promises. I miss the relationship we had years ago, before I got addicted to drugs and alcohol. Before my solution to my problems became heroin and a needle. I hate getting high, I don't understand why I keep doing it. I guess it's mainly because I don't know how to live life anymore and have no conception of reality what so ever [sic]. I'm so tired of the life I live and wishing every morning that I didn't have to wake up again. I hope I can finally recover and become half the woman you are. I'm so proud of everything you have accomplished so far, and all of the help you give to people like me who suffer every minute of every day.

Every time I think about you, Dad, and Liam, I cry. Although I can't show it, I love you guys with all of my heart. I realize I am not only doing this to myself, but the three of you also. I just want to be the daughter you both deserve and the big sister Liam should have. I hate drugs so much, I don't want to get high anymore. We both know I mean that, but words don't really mean anything anymore. But I know there is a way out besides dying. I want to find it so bad, so many over-doses and God still wants me here. I truly believe we will help

people together someday. Thank you for everything you do.
I love you.
   Katie

"That was my daughter," I tell Nikki. "She's overdosed thirteen times that she admits to and has been in more than forty treatment programs. She keeps trying, though. She's pretty amazing."

"How is she now?"

"Today is a good day, today is a very good day. Now, let's figure you out."

Nikki goes to treatment, along with Justin and Kevin, Jennifer and Brittany, Hayley, Peter, and Chris. They all go, some reluctantly at first, and some leave before they should, while others stay the course and relapse later. Too many don't make it. But then some do, and they become the Sammys and Kyles and Susannas and Gabes and Mandys and Nicks; that's what inspires me and is why I keep getting up and doing this every day. Sometimes a person's stint in treatment is the final time and I get to watch them live their lives afterward, and it's a beautiful thing. I comfort myself with the knowledge that recovery is possible.

There seems to be a vigil every night, beginning on August 31, International Overdose Awareness Day, and going through September, which is National Recovery Month.

I recall the previous year's vigil in Marlborough, when I stood with Marion, only a few months after she'd lost her only child, and spoke to Kyle's heartbroken mother, Barbara. They are unable to attend this year. Kyle is at a family function with his new wife, and Barbara is learning to live with her grief and balance it with the relief and happiness of her remaining son's success.

A prior year, Rhonda and I stood at a table covered with a purple cloth, on which were arranged brochures and wristbands and postcards, all with Magnolia's contact information, as we had done a thousand times since. This time the backdrop is the beautiful shoreline of Gloucester.

People browse the lined-up tables, where presenters are sharing their wares and hoping to connect with someone who needs help. As if losing her nineteen-year-old daughter wasn't hard enough, Rhonda is helping her twenty-seven-year-old daughter through addiction treatment for the same drug that took her sister's life.

Rhonda speaks, as she often does, in front of the crowd; she tells of her daughter Mariah, who had a beautiful spirit and a smile that lit up a room. Rhonda will bring Mariah to life in front of the crowd and show the face of addiction and the effect of the loss of a child. People have gathered from all over the North Shore of Massachusetts to come together to remember those who have been lost.

"Between the ages of fifteen and seventeen," Rhonda says, "she was in treatment five or six times and at a residential program briefly. She tried. That was the thing . . . Mariah wanted to live a 'normal life,' she wanted to be well, but that was often a struggle for her. Along the way, she was diagnosed with a major depressive disorder and severe anxiety. I still wonder how much of her drug use was self-medicating."

Across the crowd, acknowledgment registers on the faces of many, surprise on others, and fear on nearly all. Rhonda—beautiful, petite, intelligent, and incredibly together-looking—is not what you think of when you imagine the mother of two daughters affected by this disease. But she is, in fact, exactly who this heartbreak all too often strikes.

"She had been living at home," Rhonda recalls, "and working and doing well for months. She relapsed on a Saturday or Sunday and was gone by Monday, July 11, 2011. She had been doing so well, in fact, that when the police came to the door late that night, it didn't even occur to me that the worst had happened."

The strength that allows Rhonda to stand and share her story astounds me every time. And no matter how many times I hear it, it never fails to bring me, and many others, to tears. I know why she is able to continue. She carries her daughter's spirit with her because it enables her to speak up and offer comfort to others, not only by talking about Mariah but also by running grief support groups for others who have lost a child in this way. She has been a safe place and a source of support and knowledge since the first time I spoke to her. I feel honored to call her my friend. What an amazing gift to know people like her. We have bonded over such heartache that I feel as though she is a sister more than a friend.

"You need help," she says to the people gathered in the park that day. "There is so much shame and stigma associated with the disease of addiction that people often suffer alone in silence. This is starting to change but not quickly enough."

She then reads an E. E. Cummings poem I have always loved, though now it has new meaning. It truly conveys how she stands and shares this tragedy and how she continues on to help anyone who needs help, no matter how painful it is for her.

> i carry your heart with me (i carry it in
> my heart) i am never without it

There is no doubt in my mind as I look at Rhonda, silhouetted against the dusky sky, waves lapping in the distance, that she does in fact carry Mariah in her heart, that her daughter is proudly smiling at her hero of a mother. Rhonda leaves the stage and takes her place in the crowd next to me.

"You were awesome," I lean over and whisper.

"I don't believe you, but thanks anyway."

Rhonda's oldest daughter and Katie continue to struggle, but they are still with us, and where there is life, there is hope.

I call Chance to check in for the first time all day, having broken the routine of making my usual first call of the morning to her.

"There you are," she says. "I was wondering when I'd hear from you."

"It's been a day," I reply. "I'm meeting Marion for dinner."

"Oh, I wish I were closer," Chance says in her slight southern drawl.

"I wish you were closer, too, but then we would never get anything done because we would be talking all day, instead of just most of the day. What's new, anything?"

"Not really. You saw the post from the mom in Massachusetts looking for a doctor who'll give a Vivitrol shot, right?"

"Crap, yes. I'll respond as soon as I park."

"Are you in the car again? That car is more of a phone booth! Hey, I know—why don't we get you a mobile home? But don't worry about responding to the woman from Massachusetts; I've already done it."

"You're awesome, thank you. I don't think anyone realizes how much you actually do."

"We are all in this same leaky boat together, sister."

"We are, and there is no one I'd rather sink or swim with than you, my friend."

Marion gets to the restaurant about ten minutes after I do. We talk about the fund-raiser she just had in honor of her son, Brian, similar to the one we held last year for women's sober living scholarships in honor of Rhonda's daughter Mariah.

Brian's friends gathered together around his birthday to put together a basketball tournament. He, like his mother, had a way about him that made him unforgettable. They raised more than five thousand dollars and donated it to Magnolia for the Brian Murphy Sober Living Scholarship. Marion honors his memory every day by working as a recovery coach and trying to guide others into recovery. She has a special place in my heart, and I'm fiercely protective of her. She is the reason I survived this, and I know that. Had she not reached out to me that night at my first Learn to Cope meeting, I would have gone home and never returned—and would most likely have tried to deal with all of this alone, which is no way to handle a problem like this.

"You look terrific!" I say.

We've all transformed in small and big ways. I imagine it's the change that people who go through battle feel, and some of the bond as well. We have been fighting a war.

"Do you think this has gotten easier, or have we gotten tougher?" I ask.

Marion pauses for a bit and gazes into the crowd of people waiting for a seat at the bar in the adjoining room.

"I don't feel tough at all. I feel like I am getting through every day just trying to make sure not one more life is lost."

"I have an idea," I say. "Let's turn off the phones and not talk about kids or drugs—and especially not kids *on* drugs. Let's pretend for an hour or so that there's no such thing. Let's just be two friends having dinner."

"You have yourself a deal," Marion replies, smiling.

epilogue | The End of Summer 2017

The ride back from the Cape at the end of August on a Sunday is slow. Randy picked me up early on Friday morning, and we made our way down and spent the weekend looking at houses. We have a dream to live part of the year on the Cape, the other in Puerto Rico. Large backyard, near the water, outdoor shower—the shared list goes on. The light at the end of the tunnel. I glance over at him; sand still clings to his calf. I'm tempted to brush it off, then decide to allow the peaceful, languid beach day to remain with us for as long as possible.

Stopped in traffic near Route 3, I peer into the adjacent cars. A couple in their early thirties, clearly arguing, New York plates and bikes tethered to the back of their Zipcar. Do they still call them yuppies, or did I miss the evolution of a catchphrase? Perhaps the weekend away wasn't what they had hoped for, or maybe it's just the stress of returning to life after the escape from reality. I turn away from the anger, aware that I will never know the cause of it. A group of young men pass by, blasting something they think is music but sounds more like a prison riot in the making. When I lean forward to see out Randy's window, a small boy with blond curls waves through the passenger window of the vehicle in the adjacent lane, his sister asleep in the car seat next to him, lollipop still in her hand. I wave back. The mom looks over at me and smiles a smile of camaraderie. She can tell I'm contemplating a scene I've been a part of. What she doesn't know is that I'm wondering, Which child will it be? Who will break her heart, and how much pain will she need to endure? Or will she be one of the lucky ones, spared the anguish of drugs? I pray it's the latter and smile back. I rarely view children or families the way I once did. My innocence is gone. I wonder if I'll ever be able to look at a scene like that in any other way.

"How is your week shaping up?" I ask Randy.

"It's busy, but let's not think about it."

He's right. Like the sand on his calf, the day, too, should linger. I allow myself another few hours of peace and sit back and enjoy being still. I'm learning to hang on to happiness for as long as possible. Vivaldi's Largo plays quietly in the background. I don't want to move past this moment.

I had spoken to Katie on Thursday night. A text from Bob just before that had stated that she had overdosed. He'd detailed how much Narcan he had used and how he had performed CPR, expecting to be thanked. Instead, he was told to burn in hell for his part in facilitating what seems like repeated attempts at assisted suicide.

"I fucked up again, Mom," she said on the phone, after.

My answer was simple: "What are you going to do about it?"

She knows how to get herself into treatment. I can force her into treatment by sectioning her. I can threaten her into treatment by reporting her to the court—those long-ago arrests never cleared because she could never stay sober, a condition of her probation. I have done all those things before, all unsuccessfully. The key is that she needs to want it.

We have come full circle, and I know there is nothing I can really do. It's like the Serenity Prayer. I may have finally received or uncovered the wisdom to know the difference between what I can and can't change. I've come to understand what Viktor Frankl meant when he wrote in *Man's Search for Meaning*, my favorite book, "When we are no longer able to change a situation . . . we are challenged to change ourselves."

I will never give up hope, never. I made that promise to Katie. But I also won't give away my own hope. I'm no good to anyone if I don't have hope for myself.

"I don't want to go back to treatment."

I respond, "Do what you're going to do, Katie—that's what you are going to do anyway. Just know I love you."

All too aware that each time I speak to her could be the last, I always end every conversation with those words.

Walking through Marblehead, Katie and I ask together, "Which way?"

"Let's look in the windows and see whose house we want to live in!" Katie suggests.

"Okay, but don't make it as obvious as you did the last time we went for a walk. Remember? Those people almost invited you in for dinner!"

"Mom, that was years ago."

It feels good to laugh with Katie. She's so good at laughing. No more skin and bones, she is back to looking healthy. Her skin is clear, and her neatly done eyebrows tell a story themselves. She has recently colored her hair, and it is a glossy dark brown, hanging midway down her back.

"I think I'm going to go back to my hippie, earth-crunchy look," she half-told, half-asked me.

"I like that look. You drank green juice and ran a 5K on the beach when you had that look."

"I know. That seems like a million years ago, doesn't it?"

"A million and one, Ladybug. A million and one."

We walk down the street and make the left past Abbot Hall. To one side, there's a house with curved windows so strange we spent ages wondering if they were an optical illusion, until the night years ago that we hopped the fence to touch them, and prove they were not in fact flat. The dining room walls are painted red, and where artwork should hang you can peer in and see children's drawings. The pictures catch our eyes at the same time, and we smile.

"I hope I have kids someday," Katie whispers.

"Why wouldn't you?"

"Well, you know, so much has happened, I just wonder if I can."

"What would you do differently?" I ask. I guess I'm really asking what I could have done differently, but I know she will say nothing. And I know I shouldn't ask, but I do: "What will you do so that this won't happen to your children?"

"It started out small. I never felt like I fit in. I'm not sure what you could have done. First, it was trying to get really thin, to be pretty, to be accepted. Then it was the alcohol. I felt confident and started to feel like I was part of the group. I started with coke and pot, and it filled the emptiness temporarily and shut down all the noise in my head that told me I wasn't good enough."

It pains me to hear her talk like this. *Why didn't I see it when it was happening?* She seemed so much like any other teen, full of angst and hormones.

We continue on toward Old Town. It's just past seven p.m., and the sky is tinged with pink. "Red sky at night, sailors' delight," my mother used to say. I wonder if that's how my mother felt, if she drank to feel like she was okay.

We walk past a bar known to anyone who sails into Marblehead Harbor, Maddie's Sail Loft. Some of the locals are standing outside, smoking and laughing. One young guy calls out to Katie, and she walks over to say hello. She's been to more than forty rehabs, has been arrested, in jail, and has overdosed at least thirteen times by the age of twenty-four. I can't help but wonder, *Why her?* She comes back, takes my hand, and we walk toward the town dock.

"I love thinking about you and Liam going to the Y camp on Children's Island."

"That place was full of seagull poop. But it was fun, just not for the whole summer."

"One of my happiest memories is hearing the entire boat full of campers, you included, singing as you came into the harbor on the *Hannah Glover*, an old trawler, back from a day on the island. Did you feel like you didn't fit in—even then?"

"Always, for as long as I can remember. Drugs and alcohol are not my problem. I'm my problem, and only I can fix it. That's why, I'm telling you, you didn't cause this and you could never fix it. The first time we went to the hospital and you had me tested and I told you I had tried heroin and I was drinking too much, you remember? I had been drinking a box of wine a day. I should have stayed there and gone to an inpatient program. I was hallucinating and withdrawing, and they sent me home and to an outpatient program. I wish I could have caught it then. Back when I was still afraid of all that eventually happened. After heroin, homelessness, and jail, death didn't scare me. Life scared me, happiness terrified me, because that can be taken away. Misery became comfortable and predictable."

"I was so relieved they didn't think you needed an inpatient program," I recall. "I just couldn't wrap my head around the fact that you could be that bad. I didn't see it. When I looked at you—shit, when I look at you now—I just see my perfect sweet little girl. I hope you always knew that we loved you. Everything, even the crazy things, were done out of love."

"I know, Mom. My disease constantly tells me things like *you are going to relapse anyway, so you might as well do it now* or *you're not good enough for recovery, you deserve this life.* I lost hope. I hated myself, and the more I knew how I was hurting everyone else, the more I wanted to dull that pain. It's a vicious cycle. I think I'm really done, though."

When all of this started, I'd convinced myself that we would overcome her disease together. Now I realize that she is on her own journey, and I am on mine.

In Old Town, the houses are directly on the street. The roads have been widened almost up to the doors of the centuries-old homes. In one house, a man still in suit pants, his sleeves rolled up and a Labrador at his feet, is doing the dishes in the back of the house, seen through the living room window.

In another, we have to turn our heads as we are caught looking at what a family is watching on the television.

"Which house?" Katie asks, reviving our old game of Which House Do You Want to Live In?

"I think I'll keep my own," I say, pulling her close. "There's no telling what goes on behind those doors."

At the end of Front Street, before we turn back toward home, we pass a smaller house; a porch big enough to stand under in the rain covers the bright red front door. Inside, a woman in her seventies reads alone, sitting completely still. Just as we pass the window, she lifts her eyes, and they meet mine. A moment, no more, passes as we hold each other's gaze. What more will happen in the years between now and then, for me?

The traffic is flowing again; I'll be home in just a short while and will need to turn my phone on again. Back to reality. A reality somewhat altered, although nothing around me has changed, only me.

Magnolia has grown to thousands of people across the country, all seeking help and offering support, and I have learned that I am powerless, and always have been, to help my own daughter. The only person I am able truly to help is myself. The irony of that is staggering. How often have I offered the sage Al-Anon advice "you didn't cause it, you can't control it, and you can't cure it" to distraught parents, and then fought against the tide to battle the disease harder than Katie was? The sorrow of grieving for a child still alive, every day for years, has made me realize that I am not in control. I speak to her about throwing away the gift of her life, but I am doing the same.

On a constant alert for her or anyone who needs my help, I had forgotten to live my own life. Her addiction was heroin and mine was motherly love, both of them killing each of us. It was a race to see who would go first. There was a time when I prayed that it would be me, but no longer. I can clearly see that no amount of my giving up my own happiness will help her. It doesn't work that way. I want my life back.

All of the things I thought I knew run through my mind as the traffic lightens. All of those walks through Marblehead, imagining the lives of the people inside the houses. Thinking I knew why no one reached out to me after Katie's arrest or why neighbors never extended a hand in a snowstorm. Believing that my parents didn't love me because they chose drugs and alcohol over parenting, as if they had a choice. How arrogant was I to think that I could judge and ask not to be judged myself?

We turn onto I-93 and I recall the signs I didn't see: the missing money, the jewelry, and those goddamn spoons. Occasionally, I still go to use something—like the small digital camera I bought for myself as my only graduation present for my master's degree—and a new pain of loss stabs me when it's nowhere to be found. The lies upon lies that I told myself and others in Katie's defense. Watching people, mostly mothers but other family members as well, sacrifice their marriages, their jobs, and their own personal happiness, as if striking some bargain with God where they will stop living to save their child—all of this had opened my eyes. The simple truth is that you can't barter with God.

We reach the sign that announces MARBLEHEAD, BIRTHPLACE OF THE AMERICAN NAVY, then pass a house I visited recently on a call with the local police department. The town I had felt so shunned by had reached out over a year ago and invited me to join the opioid task force, a group of town officials trying to find ways to lessen the effects of the crisis. I suggested a door-knock program similar to others in the state; Gloucester, Arlington, and Methuen all had such programs. We would go out to assist those who had experienced an overdose and offer them services, including Narcan training and access to treatment. The program was seemingly a huge success, immediately reducing overdoses by helping those who needed help to find it. Accompanied by a police officer, I visited several homes in my town to offer my help. Some of them were those very houses that I had walked by wondering what I had done wrong or wishing I could trade places.

These days, I turn inward. I meditate, go to the gym, and stroll through the local bookstore to find books that aren't about addiction. I read beach books at the beach. I put down beach books at the beach and stare off, as far as I can, across the folding waves. I look out to the thin line that separates the sky from the sea. To me, there's a great hope in that crazy thin line, infinite hope, even. Everything is in that line: the rest of the world, and freedom, too. The freedom to love so completely that it, in turn, sets the lover and the beloved free.

For those born with a lurking, insidious disease, the only known cure is no first time. Beyond that, the treatment is love. So much love that it is beyond comprehension until you have been to the other side of it. And then, even then, all too often, it's not enough. But there is no harm, no foul, in love. You do not have to enable, or fix, or even be subjected to the horrible effects of the disease, but you can still let your love be known. No matter what happens to my sweet daughter or any of the other beautiful souls I have had the pleasure to know, I will never regret giving them love. I can rest knowing that they were loved.

Katie and I are almost home, done with our game of Which House Do You Want to Live In?, when she says, "Mom, what will you do if this is really it? If I never relapse again? Will you keep working to help other people? Don't you just want to get off this ride?"

Katie's big brown eyes are sparkling again. She has quit smoking and resumed running—she and Randy are back to their 5Ks, and the next one requires the wearing of Halloween costumes. On her left hand sparkles the stone of the Claddagh ring her boyfriend, John, gave her for her twenty-fifth birthday, a birthday that at times I never thought I'd see her celebrate; the stone's heart points inward, signaling to all that she is taken. She and John are working and saving money for the future. I don't know where it's going to go, but I know I am enjoying the moment with my whole being, fully.

It's a good question, actually. The day-in and day-out pain, occasionally relieved by great happiness, is draining, and I'm exhausted.

"I want to get off the ride with you, Katie. I've learned how to help people, and if I get off the ride completely, then all this pain, heartbreak, and hell we've been through is just nothing more than pain. I have to believe that we went through this so we can help someone else."

"I'd like to work with you," she says. "I want to pay it forward for all the people I know who didn't make it. I've lost so many friends. They died one after another when I was still getting high, and it hurt then, but when I look back, I know I didn't feel the losses like I do now. In the future, I want to do something that honors them and that helps people—do you know what I mean?"

I savor the word *future*. It is a beautiful word.

"Yes, sweetie, I know exactly what you mean," I say.

She doesn't yet realize that she does honor those friends, every day, and that everything I've done has been done with her in my heart.

"Look around at what you've already done," I tell her. "None of this would've happened if it weren't for the fact that I know what a beautiful person you are and that if this could happen to you, then it could happen to anyone. I think we are both finally on our own separate paths and they may come together again. Nothing would make me happier, sweetie."

Katie and I turn toward home. She will stay the night, and I will bring her to her own home in the morning. We walk past the grocery store she first worked in, past the middle school, and down the road on which she walked home every day from school.

She will sleep with me, we will eat Ben and Jerry's, and we will watch reruns in bed. If she falls asleep first, I'll watch her like I did when she was a baby. Because I can. And I know that this is a gift.

Every day is a gift. Every day is a new beginning.

Afterword: June 30, 2019

As I drive through Malden today, I recall another trip down Pleasant Street, driving Katie to a sober-living home four years ago, after bringing her back from Florida. It was a new start, a new sober house, close to me but not *too* close. She was nearly six months free of drugs. It had always been like stepping to the edge of a cliff and needing to trust there was a net below. Dangerous work. I was so full of hope and fear and worry.

I feel some version of that again today. It's strange being back here after so many years. So much has happened since that day. I'm changed in almost every way.

Just west of the Malden MBTA station we pass remnant-survivors of what was called "Doctors Row," a long-ago fashionable series of mid-nineteenth-century Victorian houses built in the 1860s. The two-and-a-half-story homes with their slate roofs, expansive bay windows, and shaded porches draw visions of the early merchants, and then, with the arrival of the railroad, the newly wealthy contractors, and then the many doctors by the 1900s. Although still standing, the houses are grittier now, and the neighborhood that bustled in its heyday is crowded and confined. The beautiful structures, restored to look as they once did, are filled with professional office spaces and cramped apartments, forever changed.

Traffic slogs along as it does every weekday and my mind drifts to the losses, the funerals after funerals. The calls from mothers and fathers and wives asking for help and guidance.

I stop at a light near my destination and think back to the day I drove, dazed and possessed, to beat Bob to death with a Louisville Slugger. It's hard not to laugh just a little at how crazy I was at that moment. Yet I still understand. If not for Katie coming out into the parking lot when she did, there could have been a very different ending.

So many people have told me that I am telling their story and share very similar tales with me. Calls, emails, and texts come in every day. I try to respond to them all quickly. I know the feeling of urgency. I thought I was the only one, but now I've realized we are all so much alike in our desperation to save our children. An impossible task, though we continue to try.

Just recently at a 5K race to raise money for the Boston Bulldogs, a local sober running club, I was speaking with a few people, and one of them mentioned Magnolia. A young woman who was volunteering at the table said, "Oh, Magnolia? I got a scholarship from them a couple of years ago."

"What is your name?" I asked.

Clearly wondering what my new interest in her could be, she hesitantly told me that her name was Kelsey.

"Oh, I think we spoke at one point. My name is Maureen."

Kelsey's face lit up like a Christmas tree, and she came forward and hugged me. She wanted to introduce me to her mother and her son, whom she had lost custody of years ago. She was now able to be his mother again and repair her relationship with her own mother. The one month had turned into many, and she identified herself as a person in long-term recovery.

This is my life now. I have an inordinate number of friends with neck tattoos. I have more "adopted" children than I could ever imagine. My house fills on holidays, and I am blessed to be a part of so many incredible people's lives. People I never would have known if it weren't for Magnolia and Katie.

The conversation with Kelsey got me thinking about the people I wrote about in the book. So many people pass away, over 72,000 a year, and the people in this book were at the lowest point in their lives. The odds that they would all be alive and sober two years later were slim to none, but that's exactly what happened. Like so many others, they recovered quietly. No headlines or fanfare. I see it every day.

I speak to many of those in the book regularly but reached out to a few of them just to see if they had anything to add to this memoir, of which they had unwittingly become a part.

Gabe Wright, who I picked up on the side of the road with all of his belongings right before New Year's in 2017, gives a response, characteristically short and sweet: "Just that you're awesome and I love you." He has reinvented himself, and it hasn't been easy. Although he has struggled, he has never gone back to heroin and works hard and is living a good life. I have had the pleasure of finding out that he is really smart and funny as hell.

Kyle, who had recently lost his own brother to an overdose, responds first with a picture of the new house he and his wife are buying. He's a busy man these days, but he promises to keep in touch. He wants people to know that if he can recover, so can they. His wife is lovely, and they deserve each other in all the best ways.

I see Mandy at every recovery event. She continues to try to live down the video of herself overdosing in the dollar store. She has reunited with some of her family and fills her time by working with people who suffer with substance use disorders. She tells me her dreams of eventually becoming part of her children's lives again—something that she has not yet been able to make happen. So she works toward being a person they'd be proud to have as a mother, and she looks toward the future. I think she's succeeding.

Susanna is finishing up some time for a parole violation but has been sober for a year and a half. Her plan is to move into sober living closer to me and start over. I regularly tell her about Katie, and I believe it gives her hope.

Sammy, the first person whom I ever helped get into treatment, runs a sober living retreat with her partner and has her son with her full-time, much like Kelsey.

All of the people I wrote about two years ago are still alive. Time and support have enabled them all to thrive and stay sober and reconnect. Certainly, very few people thought Katie would make it.

Nearly two years ago, Katie was leaving a treatment center once again. If history was any indicator of the future, she should have been using within the week, overdosing, and then going back to treatment. Riding that rollercoaster, I was always hopeful during the highs but constantly waiting for the stomach-turning plunge into the lowest of the lows.

Much to my surprise, after moving in with her boyfriend instead of into the sober house that I would have preferred, Katie immediately got a job at Dunkin Donuts, a company that gave her a chance even though she hadn't worked in a long time. I was in for another shock when she came to me for help to find a therapist. I reached out to the many wonderful people I have come to know, and my friend Michelle recommended a woman named Pip.

Pip would reveal herself to be someone who always picked up Katie's calls, cared for her clients, and was the answer to our prayers, much like Trish had once been for us.

Pip specializes in trauma and PTSD. Thanks to seeing her, along with the safety net of a monthly shot of Vivitrol—an opioid blocker that eliminates the high, reduces the cravings, and helps to prevent an overdose—Katie is sitting next to me right now.

I look over at my daughter as we drive through Malden, dressed in her school's aesthetician whites, and I know she's nervous. She is taking her licensure exam so that she can practice all of the skills she has learned in school over the last year. Katie had been asked to leave this school once when they suspected drug use and then again when she tried to go back but relapsed. All of this under my nose, but I didn't see it.

At the testing site, Katie now performs the hands-on portion of the test, giving me a facial and simulating various procedures for the proctor of the exam. I can feel her hands shaking as she applies the moisturizer. I try not to let on that I have something burning in my eye and water dripping down my back. When she is finished, she is escorted into another room and I wait for her while she completes the written portion of the exam.

I watch as hopeful test takers receive their scores, determining if they will be able to practice the skill they have trained for or if they will need to go back and try again. One young girl, who clearly has not passed, listens carefully to the directions on how to retest, and my heart breaks for her. With no way of knowing what her road to this moment has been and how she might handle the results this time, I wish her luck and hold inside a fear for her that I might not have considered before. My life is inextricably drawn into the before and after.

Katie has been studying her handmade flashcards for weeks.

When she comes out of the testing room, where she answered eighty-five multiple choice questions, her face gives no indication of whether she passed or failed. She sits down and looks at her hands.

I think about the effect that not passing might have on her after working so hard to get to this point, and I know she will be fine. The effort that she has made translates throughout her life. She is resilient, and although I am aware that she is sober one day at a time, and that each day brings new challenges, I cannot allow myself to dwell in fear. It took a while, but I now wake up grateful for the day I had with her before and hopeful for the new day ahead.

I no longer ruin the present with the fear of the past.

Katie's name is called. She looks over at me for support before getting up, and I tell her that I love her. She walks to the front desk, taking a deep breath and preparing to hear her results. After a few minutes, she gives me a thumbs-up, and every tensed muscle in my body relaxes. She did it!

We stay calm until we are out in the parking lot and away from the girl that didn't pass to do an excited happy dance. We text Mike, Katie's dad, and Randy, who she calls her "bonus dad," and then the rest of the family. Katie calls John to let him know that his fiancée is a licensed aesthetician. How many other people, we wonder as we post the news to Facebook, can we tell?

"Now, that is what recovery can accomplish," I say to her.

"And humility," she responds.

It is true. Going back years later to ask if she could return to school had been a humbling experience. She was brave, and the owner of the school was as well. Katie once thought she would never be able to overcome all that had happened in active addiction. She saw people recover but believed she was somehow so unique in her misery that she would not be able to do the same. So often, the people that sink to the lowest depths of despair are the very people that rise spectacularly, offering a beacon of light to others still suffering. Katie is one of those people.

I've come to know, without a doubt, that we are losing some of the kindest and most empathetic people on the planet to this disease because we refuse to acknowledge that there is no quick fix. We shame those addicted for seeking a way out of their pain with drugs and then refuse to support them for more than the time it takes to get the drugs out of their system, if even that. The way out of addiction may begin with detox and then some version of treatment, but it is only in the continuum of care that we will find true change and healing. To me that means including and supporting the family; longer stays in quality, affordable treatment; assistance with housing and job skills; and the recognition that the co-occurring mental health disorders need to addressed. None of this happens in twenty-eight days.

My days are very different now. I spend my time speaking about the family experience of addiction, training others, and meeting with families from all over the country as a family recovery coach and interventionist. There are no easy answers, but improving communication in the family, educating them on the disease of addiction, and teaching self-care and the value of empathy, compassion and good strong boundaries are key. The important work of recovery happens after leaving treatment and re-entering the world. The family, who often becomes as sick as the person addicted, must spend time getting healthy, too.

Of course, the other incredibly important part of my life is still running Magnolia New Beginnings, which continues to offer free peer support online for twenty to twenty-five thousand people across the world, mostly in the United States, all with a loved one who has a substance use disorder. We also have offered scholarships to hundreds of people across Massachusetts who have been referred to us by state-funded treatment centers, drug courts, and departments of corrections. Along with the applications, we receive beautiful letters from people who have no one and nothing except for a willingness to recover. We are able to help with the first four weeks of treatment, and I get to meet and speak to incredible people like Kelsey and see the same transformation that I saw in my own daughter.

People do recover, as do their families. An estimated 23.5 million people live in recovery across this country, along with everyone connected to them. It is possible.

As Katie looks forward to two years sober in a few weeks, I wonder what she thinks about all of the changes. She responds with another letter. I will save it in the same drawer, next to her letters from treatment. My daughter is, without a doubt, the strongest person I have ever known and has taught me more about life than any person, school, or other experience.

I am a very lucky woman. I always look forward to tomorrow.

Dear Mom,

I know I say this once and awhile but not nearly enough. First of all; I'm so proud of you. You help so many and never want anything in return. You're a mother to me, Melody, Ryan, and Liam and so many others who don't have that motherly figure; you're a friend, a sister (even though you're an only child), and an angel. I love you so much. I wonder how many times I have said thank you. I hope you know I mean it from the bottom of my heart.

As I watch others struggle with addiction, I don't know how you held it together. Well, after reading your book, I realized I turned you into a complete nut job. I swear I didn't mean to!

But you always seemed calm, and you always told me you loved me. The two things I needed most at that time in my life.

Thank you for being my model when I got my aesthetician's license. Even though I got toner astringent in your eye, you waited for the proctor to walk away before wiping like the boss you are!

I can always lean on you, and after almost two years clean I think you're starting to be able to lean on me. Those are the things I prayed for in detox, in jail, and even sometimes in the streets. I can't believe I'm getting these things back and I have my best friend back—which is you.

You are the most forgiving and loving person I know. Keep spreading the message and standing up to addiction for me and so many others. I think I'm ready to stand up next to you!

I love you,
Katie

Photographs

Katie at age two; I was thirty-one.

Me with Liam and Katie when he was one and she was four

Liam, Katie, and my ex-husband and their father, Mike, in Ireland in 2014 before everything came crashing down

Katie, not sober, at Red's Sandwich Shop, summer 2015

Katie's wrist with "freedom" and track marks, right before she went to detox in late fall 2016. This photo ran with the New York Times *story in January 2017.*

Katie right before her JCPenney interview. Afterward, they found out about her warrants and she relapsed months later.

Katie celebrating her twenty-fifth birthday on September 15, 2017. She is currently sober. Every day is a challenge. Every day is also a new beginning.

Resources

MAGNOLIA NEW BEGINNINGS
http://www.magnolianewbeginnings.org/

MAGNOLIA ADDICTION SUPPORT
www.facebook.com/groups/MagnoliaAddictionSupport
or @magnolianewbeginnings

MAGNOLIA RECOVERY AND CONSULTING SERVICES
www.maureencavanagh.net

RECOVERY RESEARCH INSTITUTE
https://www.recoveryanswers.org/

SHATTERPROOF
https://www.shatterproof.org/

RECOVERY REFORM NOW
https://www.recoveryreformnow.org/

THE POLICE ASSISTED ADDICTION AND RECOVERY INITIATIVE (PAARI)

www.paariusa.org

SUBSTANCE ABUSE AND MENTAL HEALTH SERVICES ADMINISTRATION

https://www.samhsa.gov/

BUDDHIST RECOVERY NETWORK

www.buddhistrecovery.org

SMART RECOVERY

https://www.smartrecovery.org/

NAR-ANON AND AL-ANON FAMILY GROUPS

https://al-anon.org/

www.nar-anon.org

LEARN TO COPE

www.learn2cope.org

ALCOHOLICS ANONYMOUS

https://www.aa.org/

NARCOTICS ANONYMOUS

https://www.na.org/

H.O.P.E.S.: UNIFIED VOICES FOR CHANGE

www.facebook.com/groups/HOPESVoices4Change

Acknowledgments

Anyone who has walked in my shoes knows that there are people in this world without whom the outcomes would be enormously different. In my life, I have been blessed with many:

Randy Mason, my cheerleader, researcher, partner, shelter in the storm, voice of reason, best friend, and love of my life. Without you, none of this would be bearable or even possible to survive.

Liam, who never flinched: you are an incredible brother and son. I am so very proud of the man you have become. You, your sisters, and brother are my silver lining in this life.

My extended family: Will, Ginger, and Donald. I am blessed.

My sisters in this nightmare and my strength in the battle: Rhonda, Marion, and Chance. I am blessed to have you in my life, along with so many others.

Mike Harvey: we are proof that people can put their children ahead of themselves, their disagreements, and even divorce, and be united in helping their children.

Liz Lanier and Candace Thornton, who have listened and cared for so many years. Thank you.

My parents, Jackie and Eddie: I finally understand.

Matt Ganem, my Cyrano and teacher. There are no words to thank you for everything you have done, so I will try to pay it forward and do as you have taught me. (When are you going to let me adopt you?)

Mike Duggan, who I am sure saved my daughter's life by making her see that there might be a way to turn it all around for the first time, and Brad Greenstein and Eli Naperstek going above and beyond for what we hope was the last time.

The moderators of Magnolia Addiction Support, who carry others while they struggle themselves. God bless you for your unselfishness.

The team at Henry Holt, including Maggie Richards, Gillian Blake, and especially Serena Jones, who seemed to have always known what I meant. I knew you were "it" the minute I met you!

Elias Altman, my agent at Aevitas Creative Management. You were the person that first realized the importance of telling this story and the good that could come from sharing my experiences, and you believed in me enough to encourage me to tell this story myself. Your never-ending guidance, support, and acting as the "calendar keeper of my life" made this book possible. You are and always will be the person that opened the door to what had only been a dream.

Kit Seelye, for telling me I should write this book, that I could write this book, and meaning it!

The Fine Arts Work Center in Provincetown, class of 2012, particularly Dean Albarelli and Billy Clem for telling me to keep writing.

Finally, to all of those committed to creating a shift in perception around substance use disorder and those affected by it. You are all amazing. Never give up hope.

About the Author

MAUREEN CAVANAGH is the founder of Magnolia New Beginnings, a national nonprofit and peer support group with over twenty-five thousand members affected by a substance use disorder, as well as a family recovery coach and educator in private practice at Magnolia Recovery and Consulting Services. She holds a master's in education and a master's in public administration, is a certified trainer for CCAR's Recovery Coach Academy and Parent Recovery Basics, and is an interventionist trained in the NAADAC-approved BRI and Arise Intervention methods. Maureen is also a national public speaker on the parent perspective of addiction and family recovery.

Maureen Cavanagh was born and raised in New York and has lived for the last twenty years on the North Shore of Massachusetts. Her most important, incredibly difficult, and treasured job has been that of a mother of four children, all very different, all very loved. In addition to her own children and many young people who have become like family to her, she is blessed to share her life with her partner, Randy; his son; and their very lovable pit bull named Stella Luna, who has spent many hours supervising the writing of this book.

You can contact her at www.maureencavanagh.net.

if you love me

A Mother's Journey Through Her Daughter's
Addiction and Recovery

By Maureen Cavanagh

ABOUT THIS GUIDE:

If You Love Me tells the story of a mother who suddenly finds herself struggling to save her daughter from the grips of substance abuse disorder. The conflicts and choices made by Maureen as a mother and an advocate raise many interesting themes for discussion. The questions below are designed to enhance your reading group's conversation about *If You Love Me*.

QUESTIONS FOR DISCUSSION:

1. What are some things that Maureen and Katie's journey has taught you about the language of substance use disorders and ways to change the stigma around them?

2. What do you think people who haven't dealt with their own, a family member's, or a friend's substance use disorder can learn from *If You Love Me*? How can the book be used as a learning tool and a resource for understanding?

3. How does the title *If You Love Me* relate to Maureen and Katie's relationship? Why do you think Maureen chose this as the title?

4. Did any of the actions taken by Maureen or Mike to get Katie into treatment surprise you? Would you have done the same if you had been in their shoes?

5. Maureen created Magnolia New Beginnings to combat the lack of support from existing organizations and for-profits. What has *If You Love Me* taught you about the state of mental health treatment and the things you can do to help correct some of the issues facing a seemingly broken system?

6. The opioid epidemic is not new, nor is it the first time that addiction to a substance has caused crisis. Why do you think these epidemics occur? Can you think of parallels between the opioid epidemic and other epidemics in recent history?

7. Do you think substance use disorder is a medical problem or a problem of willpower? How has this book changed or confirmed your thoughts?

8. After reading Maureen and Katie's story, are you hopeful for the future of substance use disorder treatment and for those you know battling the disease?

9. Family is one of the most important resources you can have when battling a substance use disorder. How do you think the presence of Maureen, Randy, and Mike in Katie's life or the absence of her brother affected her journey?

10. Maureen begins to notice that there is something wrong with Katie after the spoons in her house begin to disappear. What does this tell you about the actions of those with substance use disorders? Why do you think Maureen's tipping point was physical change that had to do with her own surroundings rather than a personal change seen in Katie's mannerisms or behaviors, and how do you think their close relationship may have prevented Maureen from noticing Katie's changes?

11. Social media is used as an outlet for Maureen as she begins her journey to learn all she can about substance use disorders to help her daughter Katie. Why do you think social media, as opposed to in-person meetings, has become such a successful way to connect with others who are experiencing similar trials? Can you think of ways that social media may also be detrimental to healing and moving forward?

12. What are some ways that you, as an individual or with your community, can help address the opioid epidemic? Can you brainstorm projects that would help raise awareness about substance use disorder or pressure your local government to step up treatment initiatives and support programs? How can you reach out to neighbors or loved ones who may be struggling to talk about these issues or get help?

Contact us at readinggroupguides@macmillanusa.com.
Don't forget to check out our monthly newsletter!
www.readinggroupgold.com

Printed in the USA
CPSIA information can be obtained
at www.ICGtesting.com
LVHW091142150724
785511LV00005B/484